WALTER BENN MICHAELS is a professor of English at the University of Illinois at Chicago. Hailed as "one of the most influential American-ists of his generation" by *The Chronicle of Higher Education*, he is the author of several books, including, most recently, *The Beauty of a Social Problem* and *The Shape of the Signifier*. His writing has appeared in *The New York Times Magazine*, *The Boston Globe*, and *n + 1*, among others. He lives in Chicago.

Additional Praise for *The Trouble with Diversity*

"This is a different line, and there's a touch of genius about it."   —*The Economist*

"A withering examination of how the celebration of cultural and ethnic difference obscures our yawning economic divide . . . This is a refreshing, angry, and important book."
—*The Atlantic*

"Over the course of this short, fast book, Michaels succeeds, beautifully, in rewriting W. E. B. Du Bois's prophetic statement that the problem of the twentieth century will be the problem of the color line. For Michaels, the problem of the twentieth and twenty-first centuries is the problem of the bottom line."   —*The Washington Post*

"In his sharply argued polemic, Michaels has produced that rarity in the present idea-starved forum of American political debate: a closely reasoned, genuinely impassioned call to revive a left politics of economic justice."
—*The New York Observer*

"Bracing . . . The greatest virtue of *The Trouble with Diversity* is the tenacity and precision with which Michaels dissects out muddled ideas about race and inequality."
—*The Nation*

"I'd nominate Walter Benn Michaels's *The Trouble with Diversity* as the best nonfiction book of 2006. No longer enfant but still terrible, Michaels has been inciting and inspiring scholars and students of American literature and culture for decades; here he turns his laser-like intelligence upon the peculiar triumph of 'diversity' as a value in the American cultural imagination, a triumph which has displaced an urgently needed class politics. Identity politics is not only bankrupt, Michaels argues; it's siphoned off our energies from focusing on inequality. Michaels is a magnificent skewerer of pieties and a tremendous arguer; some reviewers thus far have often faulted him for underestimating the persistence of racism, or sexism, but this seems to me to be missing the point. That Michaels makes so many liberals and radicals uncomfortable is one sign that he's hitting home; and this isn't some neoliberal 'gotcha' book but a witty, sharp-pronged invitation to think just how we are invested in the romance of inequality, 'culture' as balm, 'identity' as pacifier."

—Maureen N. McLane, *Critical Mass*

The
Trouble with
Diversity

How We Learned to Love Identity
and Ignore Inequality

TENTH ANNIVERSARY EDITION

Walter Benn Michaels

Picador   Metropolitan Books   Henry Holt and Company   New York

picadorusa.com • picadorbookroom.tumblr.com
twitter.com/picadorusa • facebook.com/picadorusa

Picador® is a U.S. registered trademark and is used by Henry Holt and Company under license from Pan Books Limited.

For book club information, please visit facebook.com/picadorbookclub
or e-mail marketing@picadorusa.com.

The graph on page 213 is reproduced with permission from
"The Productivity-Pay Gap," Economic Policy Institute, September 2015.

The graph on page 215 is reproduced with permission from
"Unions' Decline and the Rise of the Top 10 Percent's Share of Income,"
Economic Policy Institute, February 2015.

Designed by Meryl Sussman Levavi

The Library of Congress has cataloged the Metropolitan Books edition as follows:

Michaels, Walter Benn.
    The trouble with diversity : how we learned to love identity and ignore inequality / Walter Benn Michaels.—1st ed.
        p. cm.
Includes bibliographic references and index.
ISBN 978-0-8050-7841-1 (hardcover)
ISBN 978-1-4668-1881-1 (e-book)
1. Social classes—United States.   2. Equality—United States.
3. Multiculturalism—United States.   4. Race awareness—United States.
5. Group identity—United States.   6. Social justice—United States.
7. United States—Social conditions—21st century.   I. Title.
    HN90. S6M49 2006
    305.5'120973—dc22

                                                    2006046541

Picador Paperback ISBN 978-1-250-09933-4

Our books may be purchased in bulk for promotional, educational, or business use. Please contact your local bookseller or the Macmillan Corporate and Premium Sales Department at 1-800-221-7945, extension 5442, or by e-mail at MacmillanSpecialMarkets@macmillan.com.

First published by Metropolitan Books

First Picador Edition: June 2016

D   10   9   8

This book is for Jennifer—so necessary.

Contents

The
Trouble with
Diversity

Introduction

The rich are different from you and me" is a famous remark supposedly made by F. Scott Fitzgerald to Ernest Hemingway, although what made it famous—or at least made Hemingway famously repeat it—was not the remark itself but Hemingway's reply: "Yes, they have more money." In other words, the point of the story, as Hemingway told it, was that the rich really aren't very different from you and me. Fitzgerald's mistake, he thought, was that he mythologized or sentimentalized the rich, treating them as if they were a different kind of person instead of the same kind of person with more money. It was as if, according to Fitzgerald, what made rich people different was not what they *had*—their money—but what they *were*, "a special glamorous race."

To Hemingway, this difference—between what people owned and what they were—seemed obvious, and it was also obvious that the important thing was what they were. No one cares much about Robert Cohn's money in *The Sun Also Rises,* but everybody feels the force of the fact that he's a "race-conscious" "little kike." And whether or not it's true that Fitzgerald sentimentalized the rich and made them more glamorous than they really were, it's certainly true that he, like Hemingway, believed that the fundamental differences—the ones that really mattered—ran deeper than the question of how much money you had. That's why in *The Great Gatsby,* the fact that Gatsby has made a great deal of money isn't quite enough to win Daisy Buchanan back. Rich as he has become, he's still "Mr. Nobody from Nowhere," not Jay Gatsby but Jimmy Gatz. The change of name is what matters. One way to look at *The Great Gatsby* is as a story about a poor boy who makes good, which is to say, a poor boy who becomes rich— the so-called American dream. But *Gatsby* is not really about someone who makes a lot of money; it is instead about someone who tries and fails to change who he is. Or, more precisely, it's about someone who pretends to be something he's not; it's about Jimmy Gatz pretending to be Jay Gatsby. If, in the end, Daisy Buchanan is very different from Jimmy Gatz, it's not because she's rich and he isn't (by the end, he is) but because Fitzgerald treats them as if they really do belong to different races, as if poor boys who made a lot of money were only "passing" as rich. "We're all white here," someone says, interrupting one of Tom Buchanan's racist outbursts. Jimmy Gatz isn't quite white enough.

What's important about *The Great Gatsby,* then, is that it takes one kind of difference (the difference between the rich

and the poor) and redescribes it as another kind of difference (the difference between the white and the not-so-white).
To put the point more generally, books like *The Great Gatsby*
(and there have been a great many of them) give us a vision of
our society divided into races rather than into economic classes.
And this vision has proven to be extraordinarily attractive. Indeed, it's been so attractive that the vision has survived even
though what we used to think were the races have not. In the
1920s, racial science was in its heyday; now very few scientists
believe that there are any such things as races. But many of
those who are quick to remind us that there are no biological
entities called races are even quicker to remind us that races
have not disappeared; they should just be understood as
social entities instead. And these social entities have turned out
to be remarkably tenacious, both in ways we know are bad
and in ways we have come to think of as good. The bad ways
involve racism, the inability or refusal to accept people who
are different from us. The good ways involve just the opposite:
embracing difference, celebrating what we have come to call
diversity.

Indeed, in the United States, the commitment to appreciating diversity emerged out of the struggle against racism, and
the word *diversity* itself began to have the importance it does
for us today in 1978 when, in *Bakke v. Board of Regents,* the
Supreme Court ruled that taking into consideration the race
of an applicant to the University of California (in this case, it
was the medical school at UC Davis) was an acceptable practice if it served "the interest of diversity." The point the Court
was making here was significant. It was not asserting that

preference in admissions could be given, say, to black people because they had previously been discriminated against. It was saying instead that universities had a legitimate interest in taking race into account in exactly the same way they had a legitimate interest in taking into account what part of the country an applicant came from or what his or her nonacademic interests were. They had, in other words, a legitimate interest in having a "diverse student body," and racial diversity, like geographic diversity, could thus be an acceptable goal for an admissions policy.

Two things happened here. First, even though the concept of diversity was not originally connected with race (universities had long sought diverse student bodies without worrying about race at all), the two now came to be firmly associated. When universities publish their diversity statistics today, they're not talking about how many kids come from Oregon. My university—the University of Illinois at Chicago—is ranked as one of the most diverse in the country, but well over half the students in it come from Chicago. What the rankings measure is the number of African Americans and Asian Americans and Latinos we have, not the number of Chicagoans.

And, second, even though the concept of diversity was introduced as a kind of end run around the historical problem of racism (the whole point was that you could argue for the desirability of a diverse student body without appealing to the history of discrimination against blacks and so without getting accused by people like Alan Bakke of reverse discrimination against whites), the commitment to diversity became deeply associated with the struggle against racism. Indeed, the goal of overcoming racism, which had sometimes been identified as the goal of creating a "color-blind" society, was now reconceived as the goal of creating a diverse, that is, a color-conscious, society.[1] Instead of trying to treat people as if their race didn't matter, we would not only recognize but celebrate racial identity. Indeed, race has turned out to be a gateway drug for all kinds of identities, cultural, religious, sexual, even medical. To take what may seem like an extreme case, advocates for the disabled now urge us to stop thinking of disability as a condition to be "cured" or "eliminated" and to start thinking of it instead on the model of race: we don't think black people should want to stop being black; why do we assume the deaf want to hear?[2]

The general principle here is that our commitment to diversity has redefined the opposition to discrimination as the appreciation (rather than the elimination) of difference. So with respect to race, the idea is not just that racism is a bad thing (which of course it is) but that race itself is a good thing. Indeed, we have become so committed to the attractions of race that (as I've already suggested above and as we'll see at greater length in chapter 1) our enthusiasm for racial identity has been utterly undiminished by scientific skepticism about whether there is any such thing. Once the students in my American literature classes have taken a course in human genetics, they just stop talking about black and white and Asian races and start talking about black and European and Asian cultures instead. We love race, and we love the identities to which it has given birth.

The fundamental point of this book is to explain why this is true. The argument, in its simplest form, will be that we love race—we love identity—because we don't love class.[3] We love thinking that the differences that divide us are not the differences between those of us who have money and those who don't but are instead the differences between those of us who are black and those who are white or Asian or Latino or whatever. A world where some of us don't have enough money is a world where the differences between us present a problem: the need to get rid of inequality or to justify it. A world where some of us are black and some of us are white— or biracial or Native American or transgendered—is a world where the differences between us present a solution: appreciating our diversity. So we like to talk about the differences we can appreciate, and we don't like to talk about the ones we can't. Indeed, we don't even like to acknowledge that they exist. As survey after survey has shown, Americans are very reluctant to identify themselves as belonging to the lower class and even more reluctant to identify themselves as belonging to the upper class. The class we like is the middle class.

But the fact that we all like to think of ourselves as belonging to the same class doesn't, of course, mean that we actually do belong to the same class. In reality, we obviously and increasingly don't. "The last few decades," as *The Economist* puts it, "have seen a huge increase in inequality in America."[4] The rich *are* different from you and me, and one of the ways they're different is that they're getting richer and we're not. And while it's not surprising that most of the rich and their apologists on the intellectual right are unperturbed by this development, it is at least a little surprising that the intellectual left has managed to remain almost equally unperturbed. Giving priority to issues like affirmative action and committing itself to the celebration of difference, the intellectual left has responded to the increase in economic inequality by insisting on the importance of cultural identity. So for thirty years, while the gap between the rich and the poor has grown larger, we've been urged to respect people's identities—as if the problem of poverty would be solved if we just appreciated the poor. From the economic standpoint, however, what poor people want is not to contribute to diversity but to minimize their contribution to it—they want to stop being poor. Celebrating the diversity of American life has become the American left's way of accepting their poverty, of accepting inequality.

I have three goals in writing this book. The first is to show how our current notion of cultural diversity—trumpeted as the repudiation of racism and biological essentialism—in fact grew out of and perpetuates the very concepts it congratulates itself on having escaped. The second is to show how and why the American love affair with race—especially when you can dress race up as culture—has continued and even intensified. Almost everything we say about culture (that the significant differences between us are cultural, that such differences should be respected, that our cultural heritages should be perpetuated, that there's a value in making sure that different cultures survive) seems to me mistaken, and this book will try to show why. And the third goal is—by shifting our focus from cultural diversity to economic equality—to help alter the political terrain of contemporary American intellectual life.

In the last year, it has sometimes seemed as if this terrain might in fact be starting to change, and there has been what at least looks like the beginning of a new interest in the problem of economic inequality. Various newspapers have run series noticing the growth of inequality and the decline of class mobility; it turns out, for example, that the Gatsby-style American dream—poor boy makes good, buys beautiful, beautiful shirts—now has a better chance of coming true in Sweden than it does in America, and as good a chance of coming true in western Europe (which is to say, not very good) as it does here. So when someone like the *New York Times* columnist David Brooks observes with satisfaction that what he thinks of as the "gangsta" behavior of young black rioters in suburban France is different from equivalent behavior in the United States, because in the United States, "the gangsta fan ends up in college or in law school" but "in France the barriers to ascent are higher," his own newspaper has already pointed out his mistake. In fact, according to the *Times,* "One surprising fact about mobility is that it is not higher in the United States than in Britain or France."[5] People have begun to notice also that the intensity of interest in the race of students in our universities has coincided with more or less complete indifference to their wealth. We're getting to the point where there are more black people than poor people in elite universities (even though there are still precious few black people). And Hurricane Katrina—with its televised images of the people left to fend for themselves in a drowning New Orleans—provided both a reminder that there still are poor people in America and a vision of what the consequences of that poverty can be.

At the same time, however, the understanding of these issues has proven to be more a symptom of the problem than an actual diagnosis of it. In the *Class Matters* series of the *New York Times,* for example, the class differences that mattered most turned out to be the ones between the rich and the really rich and between the new rich and the old rich or between rich people who *choose* to save some money by shopping at Costco and rich people who *have* to save some money to shop at Chanel. Indeed, at one point in the series, the *Times* started treating class not as an issue to be addressed in addition to (much less instead of) race but as itself a version of race, as if the rich and the poor really were, as Fitzgerald thought, different races, and so as if the occasional marriage between them were a kind of interracial marriage. Indeed, the only thing missing was an account of the children of mixed (wealth) marriages, half rich, half poor, confronting a world in which they can't quite find a place. And, actually, the *Times* even provided a version of that in its profile of one of the (rare) people who has moved up in class, treating her predicament with all the pathos of the torn-between-two-worlds "not fully at ease"-in-either stories that have been a staple of American literature since the first tragic mulatta found herself at home nowhere. Americans like stories in which the big problem is whether or not you fit in. It's as if being born poor and managing to become middle-class were like being born light skinned into a dark-skinned family— too white to be black, too black to be white. Or (our favorite story of all) like being the child of immigrants, with a loyalty to two different cultures.

But classes, as I will be arguing, are not like races and

cultures, and treating them as if they were like races or cultures—different but equal—is one of our strategies for managing inequality rather than minimizing or eliminating it. White is not better than black, but rich is definitely better than poor. Poor people are an endangered species in elite universities not because the universities put quotas on them (as they did with Jews in the old days) and not even because they can't afford to go to them (Harvard will lend you or even give you the money you need to go there) but because they can't get into them. Hence the irrelevance of most of the proposed solutions to the systematic exclusion of poor people (it's actually the systematic exclusion of three quarters of the population) from elite universities, which involve ideas like increased financial aid for students who can't afford the high tuition, support systems for the few poor students who manage to end up there anyway and, in general, an effort to increase the "cultural capital" of the poor. Today, says David Brooks (who despite his Horatio Alger fantasies about "gangstas" in law school has begun to notice the predominance of rich kids), "the rich don't exploit the poor, they just out-compete them."[6] And if outcompeting people means tying their ankles together and loading them down with extra weight while hiring yourself the most expensive coaches and the best practice facilities, he's right. The entire U.S. school system, from pre-K up, is structured from the very start to enable the rich to outcompete the poor, which is to say, the race is fixed. And the kinds of solutions that might actually make a difference—financing every school district equally, abolishing private schools, making high-quality child care

available to every family—are treated as if they were positively un-American.

But it's the response to Katrina that is most illuminating for
our purposes, especially the response from the left, not from
the David Brooks right. "Let's be honest," Cornel West told
an audience at the Paul Robeson Student Center at Rutgers
University, "we live in one of the bleakest moments in the history of black people in this nation." "Look at the Super Dome,"
he went on to say, it's "a living hell for black people. It's not a
big move from the hull of the slave ship to the living hell of
the Super Dome."[7] This is what we might call the "George
Bush doesn't care about black people" interpretation of the
government's failed response to the catastrophe. But nobody
doubts that George Bush cares about Condoleezza Rice, who
is very much a black person and who is fond of pointing out
that she's been black since birth. And there are, of course, lots
of other black people—like Clarence Thomas and Thomas
Sowell and Janice Rogers Brown and, at least once upon a time,
Colin Powell—for whom George Bush almost certainly has
warm feelings. But what American liberals want is for our
conservatives to be racists. We want the black people George
Bush cares about to be "some of my best friends are black" to-
kens. We want a fictional George Bush who doesn't care about
black people rather than the George Bush we've actually got,
one who doesn't care about poor people.

Although that's not quite the right way to put it. First
because, for all I know, George Bush *does* care about poor
people; at least he cares as much about poor people as anyone
else does. What he doesn't care about—and what Bill Clinton,

judging by his eight years in office, didn't much care about, and what John Kerry, judging from his presidential campaign, doesn't much care about and what we on the so-called left, judging by our willingness to accept Kerry as the alternative to Bush, don't care about either—is taking any steps to get them to stop being poor. We would much rather get rid of racism than get rid of poverty. And we would much rather celebrate cultural diversity than seek to establish economic equality.

Indeed, diversity has become virtually a sacred concept in American life today. No one's really against it; people tend instead to differ only in their degrees of enthusiasm for it and their ingenuity in pursuing it. Microsoft, for example, is very ingenious indeed. Almost every company has the standard racial and sexual "employee relations groups," just as every college has the standard student groups: African American, Black and Latino Brotherhood, Alliance of South Asians, Chinese Adopted Sibs (this one's pretty cutting-edge) and the standard GLBTQ (the Q is for *Questioning*) support center. But (as reported in a 2003 article in *Workforce Management*) Microsoft also includes groups for "single parents, dads, Singaporean, Malaysian, Hellenic, and Brazilian employees, and one for those with attention deficit disorder." And the same article goes on to quote Patricia Pope, CEO of a diversity-management firm in Cincinnati, describing companies that "tackle other differences" like "diversity of birth order" and, most impressive of all, "diversity of thought." If it's a little hard to imagine the diversity of birth order workshops (all the oldest siblings trying to take care of each other, all the youngest competing to be the baby), it's harder still to imagine how the diversity of thought workshops go. What if the diversity of thought is about your sales plan? Are you supposed to reach agreement (but that would eliminate diversity) or celebrate disagreement (but that would eliminate the sales plan)?

Among the most enthusiastic proponents of diversity, needless to say, are the thousands of companies providing "diversity products," from diversity training (currently estimated to be a $10-billion-a-year industry) to diversity newsletters (I subscribe to *Diversity Inc.,* but there are dozens of them) to diversity rankings (my university's in the top ten) to diversity gifts and clothing—you can "show your support for multiculturalism" *and* "put an end to panty lines" with a "Diversity Rocks Classic Thong" ($9.99). The "Show Me the Money Diversity Venture Capital Conference" says what needs to be said here. But it's not all about the benjamins. There's no money for the government in proclaiming Asian Pacific American Heritage Month (it used to be just a week, but the first President Bush upgraded it) or in Women's History Month or National Disability Employment Awareness Month or Black History Month or American Indian Heritage Month (all of which, except the last, have also been upgraded from weeks to months in the last thirty years; American Indian Heritage Month was only a day). And there's no money for the Asians, Indians, blacks and women whose history gets honored.

In fact, the closest thing we have to a holiday that addresses economic inequality instead of racial or sexual identity is Labor Day, which is a product not of the multicultural cheerleading at the end of the twentieth century but of the labor unrest at the end of the nineteenth. The union workers who took a day off to protest President Grover Cleveland's deployment of twelve thousand troops to break the Pullman strike weren't campaigning to have their otherness respected. And when, in 1894, their day off was made official, the president of the American Federation of Labor, Samuel Gompers, looked forward not just to a "holiday" but to "the day to which the toilers in past centuries looked forward, when their rights and wrongs would be discussed." The idea was not that they'd celebrate their history but that they'd figure out how to build a stronger labor movement and make the dream of economic justice a reality.

Obviously, it didn't work out that way, either for labor (which is weaker than it's ever been) or for Labor Day (which mainly marks the end of summer). You get bigger crowds, a lot livelier party and a much stronger sense of solidarity for Gay Pride Day. But Gay Pride Day isn't about economic equality, and celebrating diversity shouldn't be an acceptable alternative to seeking economic equality. In an ideal universe we wouldn't be celebrating diversity at all—we wouldn't even be encouraging it—because in an ideal universe the question of who you wanted to sleep with would be a matter of concern only to you and to your loved (or unloved) ones. As would your skin color; some people might like it, some people might not, but it would have no political significance whatsoever. Diversity of skin color is something we should happily take for granted, the way we do diversity of hair color. When you go to school or to work—just like when you go to vote—the question of whether you're black or white, straight or gay, a man or a woman shouldn't matter any more than the question of whether you are blond or brunette. An important issue of social justice hangs on not discriminating against people because of their hair color or their skin color or their sexuality. No issue of social justice hangs on appreciating hair color diversity; no issue of social justice hangs on appreciating racial or cultural diversity.

If you're worried about the growing economic inequality in American life, if you suspect that there may be something unjust as well as unpleasant in the spectacle of the rich getting richer and the poor getting poorer, no cause is less worth supporting, no battle is less worth fighting than the ones we fight for diversity. While some cultural conservatives may wish that everyone should be assimilated to their fantasy of one truly American culture, and while the supposed radicals of the "tenured left" continue to struggle for what they hope will finally become a truly inclusive multiculturalism, the really radical idea of redistributing wealth becomes almost literally unthinkable. In the early 1930s, Senator Huey Long of Louisiana proposed a law making it illegal for anyone to earn more than a million dollars a year and for anyone to inherit more than five million dollars. Imagine the response if—even suitably adjusted for inflation—any senator were to propose such a law today, cutting off incomes at, say, $15 million a year and inheritances at $75 million. It's not just the numbers that wouldn't fly; it's the whole concept. Such a restriction today would seem as outrageous and unnatural as interracial—not to mention gay— marriage seemed or would have seemed then. But we don't need to purchase our progress in civil rights at the expense of a commitment to economic justice. More fundamentally still, we should not allow—or we should not continue to allow—the phantasm of respect for difference to take the place of that commitment to economic justice. In short, this book is an effort to move beyond diversity—to make it clear that the commitment to diversity is at best a distraction and at worst an essentially reactionary position—and to help put equality back on the national agenda.

◆

The first chapter begins by exploring a central contradiction in American life today, the more or less complete disconnect between what we like to believe about racial identity and what probably is the case. "Races," as the molecular anthropologist Jonathan Marks recently put it, are "like angels. Many people believe in them, devoutly. They can even tell you what properties they have. But the closer you try to examine them to discover their real nature, the more elusive they become."[8] This chapter is about the ways in which, confronted with the skepticism of scientists ("Does race exist?" asks the December 2003 *Scientific American,* and it answers, "From a purely genetic standpoint, no"), people have reinvented race as a social or cultural rather than a physiological entity. Our very notion of identity—the thing that diversity is diversity of—is a consequence of this reinvention.

While the first chapter provides an account of our attachment to the idea of race, the next two chapters provide an account of the motives for that attachment. The question they ask is why, if races don't exist and the cultures we have attempted to replace them with cannot be said to exist either, we are so determined to hang on to the idea that they do. And the answer they give is that we like the idea of cultural equality better than we like the idea of economic equality (and we like the idea of culture wars *much* better than we like the idea of class wars). These chapters show, first, how antiracism plays an essentially conservative role in American politics today and, second, how the universities—as something like the diversity avant-garde—play an equally conservative role. People like David Horowitz are always complaining that universities are hotbeds of liberalism in which conservatives can't get a job, much less a fair hearing. These chapters argue that even if Horowitz and his friends are right, true conservatives needn't worry; from their affirmative-action admissions procedures to their multicultural graduation requirements, American universities are propaganda machines that might as well have been designed to ensure that the class structure of American society remains unchallenged. Contrasting the obligations of diversity (being nice to each other) with the obligations of equality (giving up our money) these chapters focus in particular on how the commitment to diversity has turned liberalism into a program for making rich people of different skin colors and sexual orientations more "comfortable" while leaving intact the thing that makes them most comfortable of all: their wealth.

As much as we like being proud of our culture, we also like being proud of our history and being proud of the way our people (whoever we think our people are) have triumphed, or at least survived. And, conversely, we like being outraged by the bad things somebody else's people did to ours, and we like thinking that justice requires they make up—or at least apologize—for them. But if the first three chapters give us reasons to be skeptical of the category "our people" and of the links we can have to people in the past, chapter 4 gives us reasons to doubt the relevance of the past itself. The question it asks is why we should care about the past, and the answer it gives is that we shouldn't, and that our current near obsession with the importance of history is profoundly misplaced. Like the idea of diversity itself, history functions at best as a distraction from present injustices and at worst as a way of perpetuating them. Henry Ford said a long time ago, "History is bunk"; the purpose of this chapter will be to show that he was right.

The final two chapters are about the ways in which the question of identity—who you are—has come to replace not only the economic question of what you have but the political and religious questions of what you believe. The first of these chapters is on globalization and on the "indigenist" resistance to it; the second is on the rise of religious conflict and our difficulty in figuring out how to understand it. The basic idea in both is that we have come to think of disagreement as a form of prejudice (we've turned disagreement into "diversity of thought"), and thus we have come to think even of our own beliefs as expressions of who we are rather than as declarations of the truth. And the argument is that, with respect to our beliefs, it doesn't matter who we are.

Indeed, the point of this book as a whole is that the least important thing about us—our identity—is the thing we have become most committed to talking about, and that this commitment is, especially from the standpoint of a left politics, a profound mistake. What it means is that the political left—

increasingly committed to the celebration of diversity and the redress of historical grievance—has converted itself into the accomplice rather than the opponent of the right. The old Socialist leader Eugene Debs used to be criticized for being unwilling to interest himself in any social reform that didn't involve the attack on economic inequality. The situation now is almost exactly the opposite; the left today obsessively interests itself in issues that have nothing to do with economic inequality.

And, not content with pretending that our real problem is cultural difference rather than economic difference, we have also started to treat economic difference as if it *were* cultural difference. So now we're urged to be more respectful of poor people and to stop thinking of them as victims, since to treat them as victims is condescending—it denies them their "agency." And if we can stop thinking of the poor as people who have too little money and start thinking of them instead as people who have too little respect, then it's our attitude toward the poor, not their poverty, that becomes the problem to be solved, and we can focus our efforts of reform not on getting rid of classes but on getting rid of what we like to call classism. The trick, in other words, is to stop thinking of poverty as a disadvantage, and once you stop thinking of it as a disadvantage then, of course, you no longer need to worry about getting rid of it. More generally, the trick is to think of inequality as a consequence of our prejudices rather than as a consequence of our social system and thus to turn the project of creating a more egalitarian society into the project of getting people (ourselves and, especially, others) to stop being racist, sexist, classist homophobes. This book is an attack on that trick.

1

The Trouble with Race

Here are two stories, one from the end of the nineteenth century, the other from the end of the twentieth. First, the nineteenth-century one. In 1892, a young man gets on a train going from New Orleans to Covington, Louisiana. Because Louisiana trains have recently been segregated, he can enter either a coach reserved for whites or one marked COLORED. Despite the fact that he is very light skinned (he is only one-eighth black, and his lawyer would later claim "the mixture of colored blood" was not "discernible"), when he enters the one for whites, he is identified as black and the conductor asks him to leave. When he refuses, he's arrested. Since his goal is to get the practice of separating the races declared illegal, he immediately petitions for a hearing before the Louisiana Supreme Court, and then, after he loses there, he takes his case to the U.S. Supreme Court, where his lawyer argues that the state has no right to "label one citizen as white and another as colored" and that the conductor's decision to label him black was "arbitrary."[1] But he loses again. There are "physical differences" between white people and black people, the Court says, and they have different "racial instincts," and these differences justify the state of Louisiana in requiring whites and blacks to ride in different coaches. So, despite Justice John Harlan's famous dissent ("Our Constitution is color-blind . . ."), the decision in *Plessy v. Ferguson* officially inaugurates more than a half century of Jim Crow, of separate schools, separate hospitals, separate water coolers, separate everything.

Now the twentieth-century story. In 1977, a New Orleans woman named Susie Guillory Phipps (never to be as famous as Homer Plessy but important to historians of race) applies for a passport and goes to the Bureau of Vital Records to get a copy of her birth certificate. In 1977, things are a lot different than they were in 1896. Segregation is now against the law. No one, not even the Louisiana court that will in 1985 have to decide whether she's black or white, believes in Susie Phipps's "racial instincts"; in fact, the court will call the whole idea of racial classification for individuals "scientifically insupportable." And the "physical differences" that had already begun to look a little tenuous in *Plessy* (remember, Homer Plessy's "colored blood" was "not discernible") are in this case ludicrously invisible. The fair-skinned and fair-haired Phipps has lived for forty-three years as a white woman. Not until the birth certificate produced by the Bureau of Vital Records said she was "colored" had anybody ever told her different, and when the Bureau of Vital Records refuses to change her birth certificate, she, like Homer Plessy, goes to court. And, like Homer Plessy, she loses.[2]

The reason that Phipps isn't as famous as Plessy, of course, is that an entire social system—Jim Crow—wasn't riding on her case. But the point of telling both these stories is that something important was: not the persistence of segregation by race but the persistence of race itself, the conviction that we can sort different kinds of humans out by assigning them to races. Homer Plessy looked like the other people on the whites-only coach, but he was nonetheless identified—indeed, in order to get himself arrested and get the constitutional challenge to the new law started, he must have identified himself—as a black man. How else could the conductor know to arrest him? Susie Phipps wasn't identified by anybody—including herself—as a black woman, and yet she turned out to be black too. Why is Phipps black? What is race if you get to belong to one without looking like you do, without feeling like you do, and without even knowing that you do?

In an officially racist society like the one Homer Plessy lived in, this question was obviously important; you can't exclude the black people unless you know which ones they are. In our society, where the commitment is not to disrespecting but to respecting racial difference, it's just as important; you can't celebrate people's blackness unless you *can* define it. The recent history of the science of race, however, has raised doubts about whether you *can* define it, and has turned the question raised by people like Plessy and Phipps—why do they belong to the black race?—into the more general question: are there such things as races? And while this question is potentially awkward (since if there aren't any races, what differences are we respecting?), there are important ways in which the difficulty of pinning race down has worked to keep it central. As race has turned from a biological into a social fact, racial diversity has morphed into cultural diversity, and a world of cultural (rather than economic or political or even religious) differences has proven to be a very attractive one for many. From this perspective, we might even say that the more amorphous our concept of race has become, the more applicable it has become as a model for treating all difference.

Thus it's an important fact about race in America that the "physical differences" the Court alluded to in *Plessy* had, right from the start, a certain immateriality, which meant that although they were usually visible, they didn't have to be. Hemingway may have made fun of the idea that the rich belonged to a different race, but he had the more or less orthodox account of who belonged to which race and how you could tell: when, in *The Sun Also Rises*, Robert Cohn gets his nose "flattened" in a boxing match at Princeton, you know that the nose in question is supposed to be a characteristically Jewish one, and when Jake Barnes says the nose was "improved" by being flattened, you know that after the boxing match, Robert Cohn looks a little less Jewish than he did before. But you also know that he still is Jewish, and so—"funny, you don't look Jewish"—that looking Jewish and being Jewish are two different things. Indeed, as we have already seen, even when the difference between races is entirely articulated in terms of how you look—when the difference between the people in question is described as something absolutely visible, like the difference in color—looks can be deceiving. The fact that your skin is white doesn't make you white; the fact that your nose doesn't look Jewish doesn't mean you aren't Jewish. In the 1930s, the (black) writer George Schuyler wrote a very funny book called *Black No More*, which imagined a process that could turn black skin white. But it didn't make race go away; it just made it harder to find. There may be some societies in which your looks really do determine your race. It's often said that in Brazil, for example, differently colored children (one light, one dark) of the same parents can belong to different races. But that's not the way race works in America.

In America, color is only a sign (often reliable, sometimes not) of your race, and two children of the same parents—however different their skin colors—always belong to the same race. In America, race has always been on the inside. What made Homer Plessy and Susie Phipps black was not their black skin (which they didn't have) but their black blood. Except, of course, that most of Homer Plessy's blood was not black. In Louisiana in 1896, he would have been called an octoroon—he had one black great-grandparent. And Susie Phipps turned out to be even less black than Plessy; her black blood derived not from a great-grandparent but from a great-great-great-grandparent. However, that was enough. The American rule of racial identity has generally been that one drop of black blood makes a black person, and since there can only be *one* one-drop rule (you can't say that one drop of black blood makes you black and one drop of, say, Asian blood makes you Asian—what, then, do you do with someone who's both black and Asian?), the effect of the rule has been to divide the American population into two major categories: black and not-black.

This is not to say that there haven't been moments when these categories looked a little crude, and finer distinctions got put into place. Hemingway's and Fitzgerald's—the 1920s—was one of them. In the years after World War I, there was widespread hysteria about the consequences of largely unchecked eastern European immigration to the United States, and extremely respectable people wrote books like *The Rising Tide of Color Against White World-Supremacy* and *The Passing of the Great Race*—the race in question being not just white people but "Nordics," the very best white people. World War I, which they called the White Civil War, had been a disaster for Nordics. While all the blond, blue-eyed types on both sides had been bravely butchering each other at places like Verdun, the darker types—"Alpines" (not bad but not as good as Nordics) and "Mediterraneans" (barely better than Jews)—had headed to the rear and waited for the whole thing to blow over. And when it did, they got lucky. From "the breeding point of view," wrote Madison Grant (not just the author of racist tracts but a member of the Board of Trustees of the American Museum of Natural History in New York and a good friend of presidents from Teddy Roosevelt to Herbert Hoover), the real winner of the war was not the British and the Americans but "the little dark man," since he got the girl.[3] He got, that is, to breed with all the Nordic girls deprived by the war of the opportunity to breed with suitably noble (but, on account of their nobility, now dead) Nordic boys. The looming threat was thus the mongrelization of America, and the Immigration Act of 1924 (called the National Origins Act because it assigned immigration quotas by country—Sweden scored high) was the major response to this threat.

Men like Grant didn't worry that much about black people, who seemed to him even lower than Jews and so not that much of a threat. But if blacks were at the bottom of the racial scale, their blood was in its own way the most powerful, since, in case of mixture, the growing consensus, as we've already seen, was that even one drop of black blood, whatever all the other drops were, was enough to make you black. The category of mulatto disappeared from the census after 1920 because of the one-drop rule. And even now, despite the recent return of the multiracial category on the census forms, it's hard to be part black. When, for example, the self-described part African American, part Asian, part Native American, part white golfer Tiger Woods started calling himself a Cablinasian, many black people were appalled at his failure to recognize himself as a black man and pretty soon Tiger himself stopped insisting. For if the one-drop rule divides America into two groups—black and not-black—for most of American history, not-black has ended up meaning white. Jimmy Gatz may not have been white enough for Tom Buchanan, but his sons would have been white enough for Tom Buchanan's daughters. That's why the world is filled with books like *How the Irish Became White* and *How the Jews Became White* (and why someone now is or now ought to be writing *How the Asians Became White*). So when Tiger Woods didn't call himself black, it looked to black people as if he were calling himself—the only real alternative—white. Despite the occasional distractions of intrawhite difference noted above, the American racial system has in the main been a kind of machine for producing racial unity (i.e., whiteness) among people from Killarney to Vilna and for producing racial unity (i.e., blackness) among people whose skin color ranges from ebony to (like Susie Phipps's) ivory.

But what is this unity? In what way are people who have the one drop fundamentally like each other and people who don't have it fundamentally different from the people who do? Today we don't talk so much about blood anymore, we talk about genes, and we are able to trace people's ancestry with a specificity that would have amazed even the most passionate nineteenth-century aficionados of physical difference and racial instincts. But it would also have disappointed them, because it has turned out that the more we know about genetic heritage, the more skeptical most scientists have become about the idea of race. In fact, the dominant scientific view now is that race is a "myth," and that, in the words of R. W. Lewontin, "as a biological rather than a social construct, 'race' has ceased to be seen as a fundamental reality characterizing the human species."[4]

The reason for this is not, of course, that there aren't any physical differences between people. People clearly do have different skin colors and different textures of hair, and we all have ancestors who came from different places or who came out of Africa at different times. The problem is that genetic variation within populations belonging to what we call the same race is often greater than genetic variation between races. So, as Joseph Graves puts it, "a person from the Congo and a person from Mali are more likely to be genetically different from each other than either is from a person from Belgium."[5] Hence it doesn't make genetic sense to think of people from Mali and the Congo as belonging to the same race and of Belgians as belonging to a different race. On the one hand, then, there are people whose ancestors came from Belgium and people whose ancestors came from Mali and people whose ancestors came from Thailand. But, on the other hand, there isn't (at least from the scientific standpoint) any white or black or Asian race. So it's not that there aren't "physical differences" (in this sense the Court in *Plessy* had it right); it's just that there aren't physical differences between races.

This point is nicely illustrated by recent discoveries about the apparent link between disease and race. For many years, at least in the United States, sickle cell anemia has been a disease—and, of course, a disease of the blood—customarily identified with black people. But it turns out that we can't really distinguish between black people and white people (between black blood and white blood) by invoking a genetic association with sickle cell. For one thing, not all of the people we call black actually have such an association, since it is characteristic among people whose ancestors were at one point centered in parts of West and Central Africa and isn't at all associated with black people whose ancestry is elsewhere in Africa. And, for another, there are people we think of as white (i.e., certain parts of the Greek population) with whom the trait *is* associated. The unifying factor is apparently descent from people who lived where malaria was a problem, since the sickle cell trait is a variant of traits that protect against malaria. Thus, as

Adolph Reed pointedly suggests, in a country composed largely of white people from the Mediterranean and of black people from southern Africa, sickle cell would be thought of as a white disease.[6]

The same point can be made, from the opposite angle, for other groups. Tay-Sachs is supposedly a Jewish disease, but, among Jews, it's only the Ashkenazi (from eastern Europe) who are frequent carriers, and frequent carriers include non-Jewish populations like French Canadians from the area near the St. Lawrence River. In a country where the population consisted of French Canadians and Sephardic instead of Ashkenazi Jews, Tay-Sachs would be most accurately describable not as a disease Jews get but as a disease Jews don't get. More striking still, if we imagined a country composed of Ashkenazim, Sephardim and French Canadians, and we used the statistical probability of being a carrier for the Tay-Sachs gene as a marker of racial difference in our imaginary country, the question of what race you belonged to would have nothing to do with the question of whether you were Jewish. The people formerly known as Jews would belong to both races.

The problem, then, for the biology of race is that there is no genetic equivalent for racial blood, for the one drop it takes to make a black person or for the many drops it supposedly takes to make someone else. More generally, there are no physical features that all the people we call black or white or Asian or Jewish do have in common with other blacks or whites or Asians or Jews and that they can't have in common with people from supposedly different races. But this scientific critique of race as a biological entity, as widely accepted as it has been, has not produced an end to the idea that people belong to races. Just the opposite. It's "as a biological rather than a social construct" that Lewontin says races don't exist, which suggests that we might better understand races not by saying that if they don't exist in nature, they don't exist at all, but by saying instead that their existence is social instead of natural. Years ago, in *Anti-Semite and Jew*, the philosopher Jean-Paul Sartre made a version of this point by saying that "Jewishness" for the anti-Semite is like "phlogiston," the substance that eighteenth-century scientists used to think was present in all flammable (i.e., "phlogisticated") materials and that enabled them to burn (i.e., be "dephlogisticated"). By the end of the century, Lavoisier showed that there was no such thing as phlogiston, and Sartre, like Lewontin, argues that there is no such thing as "Jewishness" either. But it would be a mistake, Sartre says, to think that just because there is no physical phlogistonlike Jewishness that all Jews have in common, there are no such things as Jews. On the contrary—and this is what is meant by calling race a social fact (or, as Lewontin says, a social construct)—the Jew is not someone whose body contains Jewishness (either in the form of blood or genes); "the Jew is one whom others consider a Jew."[7]

Actually, W. E. B. Du Bois produced a version of this definition for African Americans eight years before Sartre, when he wrote in *Dusk of Dawn* (1940) that "the black man is a person who must ride Jim Crow in Georgia." And the artist and philosopher Adrian Piper more recently produced perhaps the definitive formulation. "What joins me to other blacks," she writes, "and other blacks to one another, is not a set of shared physical characteristics, for there is none that all blacks share. Rather it is the shared experience of being visually or cognitively *identified* as black."[8] And once you get identified as black (or Jewish or Asian), there's no point in telling the person who's identified you that the physical characteristics are irrelevant, that the genetic differences between you and some other blacks are greater than the genetic differences between you and some other nonblacks, and so calling you black (or Jewish or Asian) doesn't establish any further connection with some biological group (i.e., a race), but just tells you where (some of) your ancestors came from. Because to deny your race—even if you don't believe in races as biological facts—is, Piper says (and Sartre feels the same way), "shameful." Everybody, Sartre says, is born into what he calls a "situation," a set of beliefs about you and ways of treating you over which you have no control. The important thing, he thinks, is how you deal with this situation. The person whom he calls the "inauthentic Jew" tries to run away from it; he says that he's not Jewish or (since there is no physical fact of Jewishness) that no one is Jewish, that there are no such things as Jews. But the person Sartre calls the authentic Jew (or black or Asian or whatever) does just the opposite. Not only does he accept the identity his situation confers upon him; he seeks to "live it to the full." The authentic Jew "asserts his claim as a Jew."

Hence Adrian Piper, even though she doesn't believe in the shared physical characteristics of race and even though she is herself very light skinned, is prepared to assert her claim as a black person, and to do so in a pretty uncompromising way. Because she doesn't look black, she has, she says, often been in the position of associating with people (at dinner parties, say) who don't know her racial identity. And sometimes at these parties, people start making racial remarks or telling racist jokes. What to do? As she points out, "It really ruins everyone's evening" if you verbally confront the person. And you're being completely disingenuous if you just object to the racism without saying that you're black. After all, when the dinner party started you were just a black person who wasn't talking about it; now you've become a black person who's hiding it. Piper's solution (remember, she's an artist) was to make a business card, which she called *My Calling (Card) Number One: A Reactive Guerilla Performance for Dinners and Cocktail Parties.* The card says, "Dear Friend: I am black. I am sure you did not realize this when you made/laughed at/agreed with that racist remark," and it goes on to explain her "policy" of distributing such cards when called for, regretting the "discomfort" she is causing the racist in question and ending "Sincerely yours, Adrian Margaret Smith Piper." What she would do is slip it inconspicuously to the individual in question, thus declaring her blackness without destroying the party. Or, at least, without destroying it for everyone.

It might, perhaps, be objected that Piper's light skin makes her situation a little unusual (although Homer Plessy and Susie Phipps would presumably disagree). But it's not hard to imagine more common versions. When I started teaching at Berkeley, I myself was once at a dinner party, happily chatting with the wife of a senior colleague, when she suddenly started talking about how the Jews were ruining the English Department. Now I neither believe in nor practice Judaism, but it was pretty obvious that Judaism wasn't the thing she was worried about. And, in fact, modern anti-Semitism has been no more interested in the religion of the Jews than antiblack prejudice has been in the religion of African Americans. The Klan didn't care about where you went to church, and when the Nazis wanted to know if you were Jewish, they weren't inquiring about whether or not you kept kosher or attended services on Yom Kippur. Of course, they didn't have a one-drop rule for Jews (the Nuremberg regulations specified that a Jew was someone "descended from at least three grandparents who were, racially, full Jews"), but the principle was the same, and it was the principle that my dinner companion had suddenly made relevant. So I did what Sartre would have wanted me to do. I asserted my claim as a Jew and said, "But you know, Jean [name changed here to protect the guilty], I'm Jewish." Which, amazingly, didn't shut her up but did make me feel a lot better.

Except, of course, for the obvious problem. Sartre says that a Jew is someone who is considered a Jew; Adrian Piper says that you're black if you're identified as black. But the whole point of both these stories is that neither Adrian Piper nor I was being treated as anything other than your garden-variety white person. So what happens to Piper's blackness if she's never identified as black? When I assert my claim as a Jew, what exactly am I claiming?

When the Susie Phipps case went before the Louisiana Court of Appeals, two possible answers to this question emerged. One is that it's blood after all. Phipps did appear to have been the great-great-great-granddaughter of a French planter and one of his slaves, and so, by the one-drop rule, she (like Adrian Piper) was black. But, as we've already seen, the one-drop rule makes no genetic sense; indeed, even if Phipps had been dark skinned, there would be no biological reason for assigning her to the black race because there is no such thing as the black race. And the court understood that. The response it gave was not the biological essentialist one but the social constructionist one, the alternative answer to the question, What is blackness? The court agreed with Lewontin (and Sartre and Piper) that race was a "scientifically insupportable" concept and that "racial designations are purely social and cultural perceptions."[9] Replacing the one-drop rule with a no-drop rule, it didn't rely on the genealogical evidence for its decision. What it relied on instead was the birth certificate. And what the birth certificate, filled out with information provided by Phipps's mother, recorded was not the genealogical detail that Phipps had at least one black ancestor but the fact that, whatever the details of her ancestry, in her parents' eyes she was black. As were they themselves since, although they concealed their blackness from her, their own birth certificates said they too were "colored." The birth certificates all said "colored," and the birth certificates mattered not because they recorded some scientific fact but because they reported how the Phipps family saw itself; they recorded what the court called their "social and cultural perceptions." And since, in the court's view, racial identity was nothing but such perceptions, the court ruled that Susie Phipps *was* black. According to Sartre, a Jew is one whom other men consider a Jew; according to the Appellate Court of the state of Louisiana, a black woman is one whose mom considers her to be a black woman.

But what do we do when perceptions differ? Susie Phipps's parents perceived her as a black woman; she perceived herself as a white woman—why should the government take her parents' word instead of hers? If she were filling out a census form instead of applying for a passport, her word is the one that would matter. The Office of Management and Budget's guidelines for collecting census data about racial identity emphasize, just as the Louisiana court did, that "racial and ethnic data categories are social-political constructs and that they should not be interpreted as being genetic, biological, or anthropological in nature."[10] But where the Louisiana court relied on parental perceptions, the OMB has since 1980 (until then it relied on the census taker) insisted that "self-reporting or self-identification is the preferred method for collecting data on race and ethnicity." The OMB takes the Sartrean account of race as a social fact (you are what others think you are) and the Louisiana account (you are what the legally appropriate others—the census taker or your parents—think you are) and reduces them to their purest form (you are what *you* think you are).

The advantage of self-identification, the OMB thinks, is precisely that it tells you what to do in case of conflicts. Because race is a "subjective" fact about individuals, a function of perception rather than biology, who can be better positioned to know the truth about you than you? So if there's a disagreement, if there's a discrepancy between your "self-perception" and what the OMB calls (in scare quotes) " 'objective' clues" (like skin color, hair texture, etc.), self-perception wins. In fact, since when you're asked about your racial identity what you're really being asked is how you perceive yourself, your responses to questions about your racial identity are not just more likely to be accurate; they are, the OMB says, "by definition," "accurate." The OMB's idea is apparently that the question of what race you are is something like the question of whether you're in pain. The point is not just that you're better positioned than other people to know the truth (they're looking at you from the outside; you're either feeling or not feeling the pain on the inside), but that you can't in principle be mistaken. You can lie about it, but you can't be wrong about it since if you feel you're in pain, you are in pain. So if I say you don't look like you're in pain but you say (truthfully) that nevertheless it hurts, you're right—it hurts. And if I perceive you as black but you perceive yourself as white, you're right—you're white.

But what are you perceiving when you perceive yourself as white? Remember, the only reason that anyone—Sartre, the courts, the federal government—is interested in your perception of race in the first place is that they're all agreed that there is no biological fact of the matter about what race you belong to. That's why the OMB says that race is not like, say, age, and why it allows census recorders to correct the information when, for example, someone born on January 1, 1950, says on January 1, 2000, that he's thirty years old. Being fifty years old is not a social construction; you aren't fifty because people perceive you as being fifty or because you perceive yourself as being fifty. You're fifty because, however people perceive you (he looks old, he looks young, she dresses as if she thinks she's still thirty), there is some fact of the matter independent of the perception. So when the OMB asks you how old you are, it isn't asking you how old you feel. But when it asks you what race you are, that's exactly what it is asking you.

And it certainly is true that when the woman at the dinner party started in about the Jews, I started feeling pretty Jewish. Which means, what? We can have a good idea of what Susie Phipps's parents were thinking when they wrote down that their baby daughter was black. They were thinking she's black because of the black ancestor; she has at least one drop of black blood.[11] But the court said they were mistaken; there is no such thing as black blood. The reason she's black, according to the court, is that her parents thought she had black blood. So the court is insisting, first, that her parents were mistaken and, second, that their mistake should be enforced. It's not your black blood that makes you black (since, the court says, there is no such thing); it's your parents' mistaken belief in your black blood that makes you black. And what am I thinking when I tell Jean I'm Jewish? What's Adrian Piper thinking when she hands people her "I am black" calling card? We're not thinking about our genes. And we're not thinking that we've been identified as Jewish or black because we haven't and usually aren't—that's why Piper is carrying her card. What we're thinking is something like what the court thought: If my dinner partner knew me and knew my genetic heritage, she would (mistakenly) identify me as a member of the Jewish or black race. And I'm going to endorse her mistake. Hence, "Dear Friend, I am black."

The idea of race as a social construction was meant to register the fact that even if we don't any longer believe in race as a biological entity, we still treat people as if they belonged to races. Indeed, we routinely—both officially (the government does it) and unofficially (we all do it)—organize the world racially. Susie Phipps's mother would have a lot more choices filling out her birth certificate today, from WHITE and BLACK to AMERICAN INDIAN to FILIPINO to OTHER ASIAN (SPECIFY) to just plain OTHER. And she would be allowed to check as many boxes as she wanted. When you're born American, you're also born black or white or Guamanian or Chamorro.[12] But we shouldn't think that just because we keep on treating people as if they belonged to races, they somehow do, or that our treating people as if they belonged to races is its own justification. Treating race as a social fact amounts to nothing more than acknowledging that we were mistaken to think of it as a biological fact and then insisting that we ought to keep making the mistake.[13] Maybe instead we ought to stop making the mistake.

But apparently no one wants to stop making it. Often we continue to talk about races as if we knew what they were. Even more often, when race begins to seem to us a little crude, we redescribe it as culture, taking remarks like "black people are good at basketball because they can jump higher" and turning them into remarks like "basketball plays an important role in black culture." Thus we don't hear much in the United States about multiracialism (as opposed to, say, in Singapore where it's an official policy and is heavily promoted on occasions like Racial Harmony Day), but we hear a great deal about multiculturalism. And if we don't yet, like Canada, have our very own Multiculturalism Day, we do have an increasing number of Diversity Days, sponsored by individual schools and organizations, where people celebrate their different cultures. When I give a lecture on race to a group of people today—especially a group of younger people—they may not be entirely comfortable talking about their racial identities, but they've already had a lot of practice talking about their cultural identities and about the importance both of cultural memory (don't forget the Holocaust) and of heritage (don't forget the Middle Passage). They're not likely to say, for example, that they're proud of their race, but they are very proud of their culture and they think other people should be proud of their cultures too.

To some extent, then, *culture* is now being used as a virtual synonym for *racial identity* (the *multi* in *multiculturalism* has nothing to do with some people liking Mozart and other people liking the Strokes), and to some extent it's also being used as a replacement for racial identity. When, for example, the alternative to Mozart is John Coltrane and the alternative to the Strokes is Jay-Z, we are more inclined to count these differences as cultural and to characterize them as the differences between a white culture and a black one. And the point of invoking culture here is precisely to make it clear that we are not talking about the biological differences that we used wrongly to associate with race. In fact, the modern notion of culture—we might call it the anthropological notion of culture—was essentially invented as an alternative to race. Its core idea was that the significant differences between groups— differences in the way they thought and acted—were cultural *instead of* biological. So when we talk about black or white or Jewish or Native American culture, we're talking about differences in what people do and believe, not about differences in blood.

An immediate objection to this way of thinking about culture instead of race, of course, is that it just takes the old practice of racial stereotyping and renovates it in the form of cultural stereotyping. Thus Richard Ford, a Stanford law professor who writes on race, suggests that "most reasonable observers would agree that, in general, blacks are distinguished from non-blacks by some distinctive cultural practices," but reminds us that lots of supposedly black cultural traits—from eating soul food to wearing your hair in cornrows—not only are practiced by some whites but are *not* practiced by most blacks. And he makes a parallel point with respect to the idea of sexual identity. Citing a Yale law professor's account of characteristics of gay culture, he agrees with Kenji Yoshino that "sodomy, public display of same-sex affection and gay rights activism" are "plausibly" identified as "characteristic traits and affinities" of gay identity, but objects that when Yoshino extends the list to "body-building, boxer briefs and goatees," the plausibility disappears.[14]

Ford's point here is that the whole project of "trying to define group differences with sufficient formality as to produce a list of traits" is flawed and that with respect both to race and to sexuality, we shouldn't try. But what the analogy between black identity and gay identity actually shows is something a little different. The problem here is not that black people are different from each other as well as from white people and therefore that we shouldn't produce stereotypical descriptions of black culture. And it's also not that gay people are different from each other in the same way. In fact, gay people are *not* different from each other in the same way; they all have at least one thing in common: they're gay! Which is to say, they want to sleep with people who belong to the same sex they do. Wearing boxer briefs may sometimes be a sign that you are gay, gay-rights activism may be a slightly more reliable sign, but desiring people of the same sex is not a sign; it's the thing itself, the thing that the boxer briefs and the gay-rights activism are signs of. So if we ask the question what is it that makes gay people gay? (what is it that constitutes their being gay?— not what causes it?), we have an answer. We're not stereotyping gay people by saying that they all want to sleep with people of the same sex; we're defining them.

So what's the behavior that makes black people black? There is no equivalent answer. You can be black and not like Jay-Z and not wear your hair in cornrows and not eat soul food and not do any or all of the things currently or historically associated with black culture. And, conversely, there's nothing you *can* do that will make you black in the same way that same-sex desire makes gay people gay. If, starting tomorrow, the only people who listened to or performed hip-hop were white (we're already halfway there), hip-hop would be a part of white culture, and if every black kid in the country were into emo, emo would be a part of black culture. It's not the blackness of the culture that makes the people black; it's the blackness of the people that makes the culture black.[15]

Two things make the notion of culture look like an attractive alternative to race. One is that culture is learned rather than inherited (it's on the nurture side of nature/nurture); the other is that culture is a looser concept than race; not all black people have to love *The Black Album* in order for it to be a part of black culture (and some white people can love it too). The problem is that the minute we call black culture black, both these advantages disappear since in order for a sentence like "Some white people are really into black culture" to make sense, we have to have a definition of white and black people that is completely independent of their culture. Culture cannot replace our concept of race as a biological entity. Learning how to rap doesn't make you a black person; it just makes you a rapper. The problem with culture, then, is that it's utterly dependent on race. We can only say what counts as white or black or Jewish culture if we already know who the whites and blacks and Jews are.

The situation is exactly the same for the notions of heritage and memory that go along with the idea of cultural identity. Suppose, for example, that in my American literature class, I teach both Ralph Waldo Emerson's *Nature* and Frederick Douglass's *Narrative of the Life of Frederick Douglass, an American Slave*. Suppose further that sitting in the front row are a black student and a white one. Neither of them (this is not a counterfactual hypothetical) has ever read either of these books. Here's one way we could describe what's about to happen. Each student is about to be given the opportunity to do two things: learn about her own heritage and learn about someone else's heritage as well. When we read the Emerson, the white student will be learning about her heritage; when we read the Douglass, she'll learning about someone else's. And the black student will be doing the same thing in reverse.

But why should this be? Why is it that some books we've never read are supposed to count as part of our cultural heritage while other books we've also never read count as part of someone else's heritage (even though they've never read them either)? And what about if they *have* read them? We can imagine a black student raised by ex-hippie parents, forced as a child to listen to the Jefferson Airplane and the Grateful Dead and read to sleep with Thoreau and Emerson (which sent her right off). It can't really make sense to say that when she reads Emerson in my class, she's learning about someone else's heritage. To think that, we'd have to think that your cultural heritage has nothing to do with the books you actually read and has only to do instead with books that are somehow imagined as genetically appropriate for you to read. But, as successful as the Human Genome Project has been, nobody has yet located—nobody is even bothering to look for—the Emerson gene.

Furthermore, even if there were an Emerson gene, it wouldn't make sense of our concept of cultural heritage, since it would of course be reproduction not instruction that kept *Nature* in the canon. The things we do have genes for—like sickle cell anemia and Tay-Sachs disease—are part of our genetic heritage, not our cultural heritage, and our genetic heritage is not the sort of thing it makes sense to be proud of or ashamed of, not the sort of thing we can be true to or give up. When people worry about losing their culture, they aren't worrying about the gene pool. In Quebec, for example, French speakers are worried that their language and their culture more generally will disappear, that French-speaking Canada will be utterly assimilated to English-speaking Canada. Hence their demand that public life in Quebec be carried on in French, and that the use of English be minimized; it provides an incentive for their children to keep speaking French instead of (or at least in addition to) English. But if there were a biological link between the French language and their children, their worry would make no sense. We don't worry, for example, that a child whose genetic heritage has destined him to be tall will, surrounded by short people, be assimilated into shortness. And, to turn the example around, we wouldn't think that if a child genetically slated for shortness managed (by eating the right foods or taking growth hormones) to get tall, he had betrayed his shortness. The dramas of assimilation—the demand that we be loyal to our heritage, the fear that we will fall away from it—depend precisely upon it *not* being biological.

It's not hard to see the general problem here. On the one hand, there are physical connections between us and the past that distinguish us from one another: your ancestors are not my ancestors. On the other hand, we can't really get much cultural mileage out of these connections. If your ancestors lived in the tropics and mine lived in eastern Europe, you're more likely to be born with sickle cell and I'm more likely to get Tay-Sachs. And you're also more likely to be taught Bantu than Yiddish, whereas for me it's the other way around. But you're not more likely to be born speaking Bantu, and I'm not more likely to be born speaking Yiddish.[16] We may inherit our diseases from our ancestors and our eye colors and our hair texture, but we don't inherit our languages. And, naturally, what goes for languages goes also for books and music and art.

If none of the students in my class has read either Emerson or Douglass and if biology can't connect the white ones with Emerson or the black ones with Douglass, what sense does it make to say either one belongs to their heritage? Indeed, does it really make sense to say there is any such thing as heritage? There are some things we inherit (our genes), and there are some things we learn (maybe Bantu or English, Emerson and Douglass). But there's no necessary connection between them. There's no reason why people with a certain set of genes ought to be reading a certain set of books and thinking of those books as part of their heritage, or why, when they read some other set of books, they should think of them as part of someone else's heritage.[17] There are just the things we learn and the things we don't learn, the things we do and the things we don't do.

We can make the same point about cultural identity, about acting black or white or Asian or Jewish. If, say, acting black (belonging to black culture) were truly a function of being black (having a biologically black body), then people who had black bodies would inevitably act black, and we would have no need for the notion of cultural identity. Acting black would be like acting tall (you can reach high things) or short (you can't reach high things). But as we have seen, we need the idea of black culture precisely because being black is not a physical fact in the way that being tall or short is. So, on the one hand, it's because there's no physical fact of blackness that, if we want to hang on to the idea of blackness, we need the idea of black culture, but, on the other, it's also because there's no physical fact of blackness that we can't hang on to the idea of black culture. Why? Because once we separate cultural diversity from racial diversity (the audiences at concerts may have different-color skins, but they are by definition not *culturally* diverse), we see that cultural diversity cannot serve as a stand-in for racial diversity. There are no boxes for musical taste on your birth certificate. You can't keep race alive by translating it into culture. We do it, but it makes no sense. Either race is a physical fact, dividing human beings into biologically significant differences, or there is no such thing as race, whatever it's called.

The American version of Sartre's "the Jew is one whom others consider a Jew" was produced, as we have already noted, by W. E. B. Du Bois in 1940 when he wrote that "the black man is a person who must ride Jim Crow in Georgia." But the beliefs about race that underlay the Jim Crow laws have turned out to be mistaken; we no longer believe them, and we no longer have Jim Crow. So the true meaning of Du Bois's definition should now be clear; if a black man is a man who has to ride Jim Crow, now that no one has to ride Jim Crow, there is no such thing as a black man. Or a white man either. There are people with different colors of skin, different textures of hair, different heights and different weights, different kinds of abilities and different kinds of disabilities. But there are no people of different races.

Which is a conclusion that no one wants to accept. Even those (the vast majority) who are critical of racism and who do not believe in the biology of racial identity have continued to insist that race is a central and even desirable factor in American life. Thus in what is certainly the most influential academic text on the social construction of race (*Racial Formation in the United States*), Michael Omi and Howard Winant write that there are two "temptations" to be avoided in thinking about race. The first is the temptation to think of it as something "fixed, concrete and objective," that is, a physical fact. The second is the temptation to think of it as a "mere illusion," which "an ideal social order would eliminate." "Race," they say, "will *always* be at the center of the American experience," and it's a good thing too because "without a racial identity, one is in danger of having no identity."[18] What we've seen in this chapter are some of the ways in which people have gone about trying to make sure that Omi and Winant's prediction comes true and to guarantee that even if people can't belong to concrete and objective races, they can still have (social or cultural) racial identities. And what we've also begun to see is how our commitment to diversity is deeply tied to keeping race alive, partly because diversity is itself understood as racial and partly because (as subsequent chapters will make clear) our commitment to diversity even with nonracialized groups (above all cultures) depends on treating them as if they were races— different but equal, worthy of our respect.

What we haven't seen is why. Why are we so eager to keep race at the center of the American experience? Why does racial difference remain so important to us when the racism it was used to justify is so widely condemned and when the basic idea about race that gave it its power—the idea that there are fundamental physical or cultural differences between people that line up with our division of them into black, white, et cetera—has been discredited? Why are we so desperate to have identities that we continue to care about them even when they get reduced to nothing more than the proud boast that you belong to a population with a 1 in 27 chance of being a carrier for the Tay-Sachs gene? The next chapter begins to answer those questions.

2

Our Favorite Victims

The most powerful scenes in Philip Roth's recent and very well-received novel, *The Plot Against America*, take place in Washington, D.C. The novel, as even those who haven't read it are likely to know, is an alternative or counterfactual history, one that imagines the American past along the same lines that Sinclair Lewis imagined the future in his 1935 *It Can't Happen Here*: the central idea of both books is a United States that follows in Nazi Germany's footsteps. But where anti-Semitism is only one weapon in the arsenal of Lewis's dictator, it's absolutely central to Roth's President Charles Lindbergh. Lewis, after all, was writing before Auschwitz and Dachau, at a time when racism seemed just one aspect of Nazi ideology. But Roth is writing in the wake of the Holocaust. And so the scenes I'm referring to involve the Roth family's experience first at the Lincoln Memorial where, reading aloud the phrase "All men are created equal," Mr. Roth is called "a loudmouth Jew" and, second, at the hotel where he and his family are told their reservations are no good and are refused a room. When the police are called, rather than setting things right, they throw the family out. "What happened?" whispers the fictional little Philip to his brother. "Anti-Semitism," the brother whispers back.[1]

Roth's idea is that it very easily could have happened here—if, say, the antiwar as well as anti-Semitic Lindbergh had actually been pushed to run for the presidency in 1940 by his friend and fellow anti-Semite Henry Ford, and if the popularity of Lindbergh's antiwar platform had helped to legitimate his anti-Semitism. So part of the book's power derives from its realism, the fact that it feels like the truth (one reviewer called it Roth's "most believable book in years"), while another part derives from the fact that, of course, it's not true (when the police come to remove the Jews from the hotel, it's scary but, like a horror movie, pleasurably scary, because its history is counterfactual—it didn't happen here). And both these facts—that it could have happened here and that it didn't—are given additional power by a third fact: that it did happen here, only not to the Jews.

It has surely occurred to every reader of this novel that its distinctive set pieces—above all the scene in which the Roths are denied rooms at the hotel—were a standard feature of American life at least from 1896 (when the Supreme Court's decision in *Plessy v. Ferguson* legalized segregation) until the early 1960s. But, as we know, it happened to black people. Which doesn't mean that there was no discrimination against Jews. Roth reminds us, for example, of the "quotas" that kept "Jewish admissions to a minimum in colleges and professional schools," not to mention country clubs. (And the memory of these quotas has usefully functioned to keep universities today from imposing limits on Asian American students.) But, of course, you didn't then (and you don't now) need quotas to keep down the numbers of black people in universities. The effects of several centuries of slavery and a half century of apartheid have made artificial limits entirely supererogatory. And, on the other side, no American Jews have ever been forced to ride in the Jew car on railroad trains, or use the restrooms and drinking fountains set aside for Jews, or gone to the special (separate but not at all equal) schools for Jews.[2] So when Mr. Roth reminds the desk clerk that he and his family have spent the afternoon at the Lincoln Memorial and quotes to him from the Gettysburg Address—"All men are created equal"— the meaning of his (not to mention the author's) outrage is clear, but the author's expectation that we will share it is a little opaque. Why should we be outraged by what didn't happen rather than by what did? How is it that we have been persuaded that anti-Semitism is an American phenomenon?

The same question might be asked about another recent work that imagines an America divided not into blacks and whites but into Jews and non-Jews. Art Spiegelman's fabulously successful *Maus* moves back and forth between Europe under the Nazis and the United States in the 1980s, famously depicting its Jews as mice, its Germans as cats, its Poles as pigs, and so on. Americans are dogs. The picture this gives of nationality in Europe is a plausible one (each country has its own different animal), but the picture of America is at least as counterfactual as Roth's. In Spiegelman's America, every immigrant group—German cats, Polish pigs, even blacks—has been assimilated, with the exception of the Jews! The German cats are now dogs, the Polish pigs are now dogs, blacks are black dogs, but the Jews are still mice. It's almost as if the Nazi racial system were an American rather than a European phenomenon. And, of course, this Americanizing of the Holocaust is not just a fictional event. Why is there a federally funded U.S. Holocaust Memorial Museum on the Mall in Washington, D.C.? In what sense—except the Roth/Spiegelman counterfactual one—is the Holocaust part of American history?

The point of the question is sharpened if one imagines a black person asking it. In his epilogue to *The Autobiography of Malcolm X*, Alex Haley tells the story of going out to Kennedy Airport to meet with Malcolm X while Malcolm was between flights and of the two of them watching some newly disembarked children "romp[ing] and play[ing], exclaiming in another language." "By tomorrow night," Malcolm said, "they'll know how to say their first English word—*nigger*."[3] Haley tells the story as a reminder of the way in which Malcolm X "never lost his racial perspective," but its real significance is more powerful. Malcolm's thought is not that the children will, in the United States, quickly learn to become racists; it's that, merely by arriving in the United States, the children, wherever they're from, will instantly become the beneficiaries of racism. They will discover what the most despised Yid from the most pogrom-ridden shtetl in the most backward part of eastern Europe (my great-grandfather, for example) discovered when he arrived in New York or Chicago: that he was a white guy. The idea, in other words, is not that Jews in the United States are—like Art's survivor father muttering about the *schwartzes*—racist; it's that they are—like Art himself, despite his mouse costume—white.

Hence it's not surprising that some of the most famous—and certainly, influential—American racists have not been anti-Semitic, or that some of them have been positively philo-Semitic. Thomas Dixon, who wrote the bestselling *The Leopard's Spots* (1902) and *The Clansman* (1905), loved Jews as much as he hated blacks, writing both against restrictions on immigration and in favor of the old plan to ship blacks back to Africa. The climactic moments in his Clan books are lynchings, which serve as occasions for people to transcend the superficial differences that divide them and gather under the banner of the one important thing that unites them: their whiteness. The "Celt," the "Viking," the "Norman," the "Spartan," the "Roman"—they all share the same "heritage of blood."[4] Even the Jews are white! In the last of Dixon's Clan books, *The Traitor*, while the carpetbaggers and Negroes lead the Clan's heroic leader away to jail, the local pawnbroker (Old Nickaroshinski from Poland) slips him a hundred dollars and whispers to him, "Don't you vorry, me poy, we'll puild a monumendt to you in de public squvare yedt."[5] The dialect that looks as if it's meant to emphasize Jewish difference is meant instead to do just the opposite. The Jew may talk a little funny and he may be engaged in his stereotypical trade, but, as a "refugee from Poland," Dixon says, "his instinctive sympathies had always been with the oppressed people of the South" (meaning the white people), and his accent marks only the kind of transitional difference that the accents of the Irish, the Swedes, the Italians and Malcolm X's romping children mark. The crucial thing is that the blood of the Hebrews is just as white as that of the Normans, Celts, Spartans and Vikings. Dixon's Jewish Clansman makes Malcolm X's point: the Irish, the Italians, the Greeks, the Jews—they are all made white by their arrival in America, and what makes them white is the presence of the "nigger."

So if it's not surprising that some of the worst Negrophobes like Jews, it's also not so surprising that the relatively recent emergence of the Holocaust as an event in American history has produced a certain exasperation among African Americans, memorably expressed by the notorious black racist Khalid Muhammad when, in the wake of a visit to the U.S. Holocaust Memorial Museum, he told an audience at Howard University in April 1994 that "the black holocaust was 100 times worse than the so-called Jew Holocaust. You say you lost 6 million we question that, but we lost 600 million. Schindler's List," as Muhammad put it, "is really a swindler's list."[6] The force of these remarks consists not in the absurd Holocaust denial but in the point—made precisely by his visit to the Holocaust Museum—that commemoration of the Nazi murder of the Jews on the Mall was in fact another kind of Holocaust denial, or, more precisely, the denial of another Holocaust. Why should what the Germans did to the Jews be treated as a crucial event in American history, especially when—given the absence of any commemoration of American racism on the Mall—what Americans did to black people is not?[7]

From this perspective, Roth's inevitable reference to the lynching of Leo Frank (every American Jew knows this name)— "You never heard of Leo Frank? You never heard of the Jew they lynched in Georgia because of that little factory girl?"— adds insult to injury. Leo Frank was the superintendent of the National Pencil Company in Atlanta, wrongly convicted of raping and murdering one of his employees, a fourteen-year-old girl, and lynched by a mob that feared his sentence would be commuted. Approximately 3,500 black people were lynched in America between 1880 and 1930; Frank was one of four Jews lynched in the same period (or ever). There were more Italians lynched than Jews; there were more generic white guys lynched than Jews.[8] But the story of Frank as an emblem of anti-Semitism in American life lives on: David Mamet recently wrote a novel about him, and in 2004, the year before *The Plot Against America* came out, so did a new history of the event (*And the Dead Shall Rise* by Steve Oney). *The Plot Against America* may be counterfactual, but it tells a story that—embodied in the martyrdom of Leo Frank and in the construction of the U.S. Holocaust Memorial Museum—many of us treat as if it *were* true. It's believable because we think of anti-Semitism as a significant factor in American history and of the success of Jews in American life as a tribute to the ways in which Jews and America itself overcame that anti-Semitism. But this is false. Compared to Negrophobia, anti-Semitism was never a very significant factor in American life. The fact that Jews were white was almost always more important than the fact that they were Jewish, and Jewish success in America today is less an effect of the triumph over racism than it is an effect of the triumph of racism.

The interesting thing about *The Plot Against America*, then, is that it portrays people who were among the beneficiaries of American racism (American Jews) as if they were instead its victims.[9] Which, of course, Leo Frank, at least in part, was. The Populist Tom Watson, whose newspaper, *The Jeffersonian*, led the attack on Frank that culminated in his lynching, never lost an opportunity to refer to him as the "rich Jew." And although Watson's anti-Semitism was much less clear than his notorious Negrophobia—indeed, a few years later Watson attacked Henry Ford's senatorial candidacy on the grounds that Ford's anti-Semitism called into question his "fitness" to be a senator—there can be no doubt that the "Jew" part of "rich Jew" had its role to play in his polemic. But there can be no doubt either about the role played by the "rich" part. What the Frank case showed, Watson claimed, was "how the capitalists of Big Money regard the poor man's daughter," and although Frank was the superintendent, not the owner, of the pencil factory in which Mary Phagan worked (his uncle, the confederate veteran Moses Frank, was the owner), he earned $180 a week plus a share of the profits.[10] Mary earned ten cents an hour; even working her normal fifty-five hours a week, she would only make $5.50. (And due to a shortage of materials which required her to cut back her hours that week, the pay envelope she was going to pick up on the day she was murdered "contained just $1.20.")[11] Her stepfather earned twenty cents an hour, which would have brought about $10 for "a normal work week."[12] So Frank made about thirty-five times what Mary made and about eighteen times what her stepfather made. Of course, this may not sound so bad by twenty-first-century standards. According to *United for a Fair Economy*, the ratio of CEO pay to the pay of the average worker in 2004 (the most recent year for which we have figures) was 431:1. In 2003, it was 301:1. In 1982, it was just 42:1. Where Mary's stepfather took home $10 a week, today's average worker takes home about $520; where Leo Frank took home $180 a week (his uncle would have been making the real money), today's CEO takes home over $200,000.[13] But in an era less accustomed to and less acquiescent in unequal distributions of wealth, Leo Frank the capitalist was at least as much disliked as Leo Frank the Jew.

When, however, Roth says of the "Frank case" that it is "only a part of the history" he's writing, a history that "goes back farther than that," it's the history of anti-Semitism that he means, not the history of class struggle, and it's Jews, not senior management, who are the central figures in this history. Or rather, since Jews, as we have already noted, are by no means the only or even the most frequent victims of American racism, it's Jews and blacks and Native Americans and Asians, not workers or managers or doctors or lawyers. For if one way of reading Roth is as someone who depicts a society that in reality discriminated against black people as one that discriminated against Jews instead, we can now see that, understood more generously, Roth's anti-Semitism is not a replacement for anti-black prejudice but a placeholder for prejudice of all kinds: antiblack, antigay, anti-Latino, antiwhatever. The point of a novel like *The Plot Against America* is to insist that racism is the problem and that it's not just Jews but the very idea of America that's the target of anti-Semites, that anti-Semitism is actually a kind of anti-Americanism, because America is—or ought to be—a society without prejudice. And this sense that we must be vigilantly on guard against prejudice is by no means limited to novels or even to the supposedly politically correct campuses where those novels get read and discussed. When in the fifth year of a conservative Republican administration, the federal government proclaims its commitment to "workforce diversity," defines *diversity* as "including, but not limited to, race, religion, color, gender, national origin, disability" and "sexual orientation," and then publishes a strategic plan "designed to increase the participation rate of women, minorities and people with disabilities," you know that a book like *The Plot Against America* has captured the temper of the times.[14] In fact, you can see why it's called *The Plot Against America*. If even right-wing Republicans like Gale Norton are telling you that you can't discriminate against people on the basis of their sexual orientation, antidiscrimination isn't just for liberals anymore.

Indeed, the Department of Interior's inclusion of sexual orientation and disability reflects a widespread expansion of the categories of diversity. When, for example, in 1968 the idea of hate crimes (now defined by the FBI as crimes "motivated in whole or in part by a bias against the victim's perceived race, religion, ethnicity, sexual orientation, or disability")[15] first entered American law, it was only crimes based on race that people were concerned with. It wasn't until 1990, when the Hate Crimes Statistics Act charged the FBI with collecting and reporting hate data, that sexual orientation began to count. And it wasn't until 1997 that the FBI added on disability. But what both the core concept of the hate crime and its expanded uses get right is that its victims, like Roth's victims, are victims of "bias."

From this standpoint, the Holocaust is the paradigmatic

hate crime, which is in part what accounts for the fact that groups other than Jews understand themselves to have been victimized along parallel lines. Thus Toni Morrison dedicates her novel *Beloved* to the "sixty million and more" victims of slavery and the Middle Passage, and Leslie Marmon Silko, in the novel *Almanac of the Dead*, reminds us of the 60 million Native Americans eliminated by Europeans. They aren't just engaging in a kind of victimization one-upsmanship. They aren't trying to replace the Jews; they're trying to join them. And the effort is no longer limited to ethnicities. The burning of somewhere between sixty thousand and several million— depending on whom you ask—witches in medieval Europe is sometimes called "the holocaust of women"; the memoir of the AIDS activist Larry Kramer is called *Reports from the Holocaust*, and the cochlear implant, designed to cure deafness, is sometimes referred to by deaf activists as a form of "cultural genocide." And it would be a mistake to think that these admittedly fringe uses of the concept are merely a trivialization of it. On the contrary, they reflect an understanding that the Holocaust is important not merely because it involves great crime (mass murder) but because it involves crimes of a certain kind (the extermination of a people). Genocides—all hate crimes—are crimes of identity, and we live in a world that is vigilantly (and, given our history, understandably) on guard against crimes of identity.

This is why it's Leo Frank's Jewishness rather than his wealth that makes him plausible as a victim and why it's racism, not money, that seems to matter. Indeed, one of the most important and even alluring facts about racism is that even

CEOs and doctors and lawyers can be its victims. No scene more vividly captures this phenomenon than the famous and controversial train chapter in Charles Chesnutt's novel *The Marrow of Tradition*, written in 1901, a few years after the decision in *Plessy*. Two doctors, a black one and a white one, friends and colleagues back in Boston, are traveling south together. When they reach the Virginia border, the conductor tells the black one that the car he's riding in is now for whites only and he is made to move to the colored car, where he finds himself among a group of what Chesnutt calls "noisy, loquacious, happy, dirty and malodorous" "farm laborers."[16] It's true that they are "his people," the doctor thinks—and by "his people," he means, of course, that they are black like him—but, "apart" from what he calls "the mere matter of racial sympathy," he finds them "just as offensive" as the whites back in the white-only car do. And he wishes that the "classification of passengers" on the trains "might be made upon some more logical and considerate basis than a mere, arbitrary, tactless, and, by the very nature of things, brutal drawing of the color line."

What makes this scene memorable is its display of the pure power of racism; it's the mere fact of Dr. Miller's blackness that relegates him to the second-class car and to second-class citizenship. What has made it controversial is Dr. Miller's sense not only that black people shouldn't be treated as second-class citizens but that he shouldn't be made to ride in the second-class car. Even the most sympathetic critics have tended to think of his response to being sent back to the colored car—in effect, I don't want to ride with these people any more than you do—as failing to demonstrate a proper sense of what he calls "racial sympathy" and of what they call "racial solidarity." And at least one way to read the rest of the novel, with its climactic race riot featuring the heroic death of one of the "malodorous" farm laborers, is as a lesson in how to build up that racial sympathy and solidarity, a sort of sentimental education for blacks required to live under Jim Crow. By the end of the novel, Dr. Miller's identification with "his people" will be a lot stronger than it is at the beginning, and the color line will look at least a little less arbitrary. Indeed we might say that the sentimental history of Jim Crow and its legacy is in general a history of the ways in which the color line has been made to look less and less arbitrary, and has instead been made to look foundational, as if the most important thing about Dr. Miller really is what the conductor says it is: that he is "colored."

As opposed to, say, that he's a doctor. We've already seen how membership in Dixon's Clan turns the ethnic differences between Clansmen into a unifying whiteness, and we can see now that apartheid has a similar effect on class. "The rich and the poor, the learned and the ignorant, the banker and the blacksmith, the great and the small, they were all one now," Dixon says of the lynch mob on its way to burn a black rapist. What's central here is the idea (passionately believed by white racists and increasingly an article of faith among their black victims) that racial identity trumps class as well as ethnic difference, so that the white doctor and the white sharecropper have more in common with each other than the white doctor would with a black doctor or the white sharecropper with a black one. Which is precisely what Chesnutt's Dr. Miller is objecting to. His point is that the doctor—as doctor—doesn't belong to a race, and if there's a line to be drawn between him and the other passengers, it should not be the arbitrary and illogical color line but rather the "more logical" method of classification the text hopes for. Indeed, that classification is the one already in place before the train arrives in Virginia (and it's the classification that resisted Jim Crow laws the longest). Its method is economic: it divides the world not into black and white or white and Jew but into first class and coach, into rich and poor. And its logic is the logic of the market: you get what you are willing and able to pay for. The color line, from this standpoint, is arbitrary because it interferes with the efficiency of the market. And, by the same token, Chesnutt criticizes the state that enforces Jim Crow as insufficiently liberal, since its police power is invoked against rather than on behalf of what he himself called "liberty of contract"—his right to buy whatever ticket he wants.

If, however, we look at the history of American apartheid, we will remember that money didn't always function as an alternative to race; sometimes it was a way of insisting on race. The poll tax, for example, was one of several devices used in the South for precisely the purpose of drawing the color line where it was no longer legal to do so. The Fourteenth Amendment had made it unconstitutional to keep black people from voting because they were black, but it did not (and would not until the passage of the Twenty-fourth Amendment in 1964) make it illegal to charge a fee for voting. The poll tax could thus be used to deny most black people the right to vote not because they were black but (ostensibly) because they were poor. And if, in theory, the law applied to poor whites too, the infamous "grandfather" clause set that right. You were exempt from paying the tax if you could prove your grandfather had voted, a test that the children and grandchildren of slaves could never pass. So the supposedly race-neutral poll tax was in fact one of the first in over a century's worth of color-blind efforts to draw the color line. And as the civil rights movement not only undid the apparatus of state-sponsored discrimination but made serious inroads into the technologies of private discrimination as well, charging people a lot of money (for your food, your school, your golf course and tennis courts) would be a handy way of enforcing the racialized hierarchies of American life. The reason you can't get in here is not that your skin is the wrong color; it's that your bank account is too small. OUR PRICES DISCRIMINATE BECAUSE WE CAN'T, reads the sign at what an old episode of *The Simpsons* calls "the rich people's mall." What the state now refuses to do, the market will do for it.

Part of the joke in *The Simpsons,* then, is the way the banner tells the truth about racism: high prices can achieve what the law forbids. But the real joke is the way in which the banner tells a quite different truth, not so much about racism as about the new irrelevance of racism. After all, it's the rich people's mall, not the white people's mall, and the monetarization of the technology of discrimination involves not just a new way of keeping the wrong people out but a new description of who the wrong people are—not the blacks, not the Jews, but the poor. It's as if the poll tax were being applied but without the grandfather clause. And when the point is put this way, we can go one step farther and see that the whole idea of the wrong people has become irrelevant. High prices aren't a clever way of keeping out the poor. The purpose of charging high prices is not to find an indirect way of excluding those whom the law no longer allows you to exclude. People who can't afford to ride in first class, people who shop at (not to mention work at) Wal-Mart instead of at the rich people's mall, are the victims of poverty, not of prejudice. This is what Chesnutt means when he suggests that the money line is less arbitrary, more logical than the color line. No one even needs to draw the money line; it draws itself.

That's why, for Chesnutt, the problem with segregation is that it interferes with "liberty of contract." And although, at the beginning of the twentieth century, segregation wasn't a problem for most Americans or for the Supreme Court, interference with freedom of contract was. In a famous case of 1905, for example, the Court struck down a New York state law that prohibited employees in bakeries from being "required or permitted" to work more than ten hours a day or sixty hours a week. Joseph Lochner, the owner of Lochner's Home Bakery, had been fined for overworking an employee, and on appeal the Court overturned his conviction, declaring that the Bakeshop Act infringed upon "the right of the individual to labor for such time as he may choose" and thereby violated both employer's and employee's "liberty of contract."[17] When Chesnutt protests against the infringement on his doctor's ability to ride in the first-class car, he is just asking that black doctors be guaranteed the same freedoms as white bakers.

By contrast, no one's liberty of contract is violated when

poor people don't shop at the rich people's mall. Rather, the poor people who decline to shop there are like bakers who decide not to work for Lochner. They're just exercising their freedom of contract—in this case, by refusing to enter into one. If you don't like the hours, you don't have to take the job; if you don't like the price, you don't have to buy the product. The injustice in Chesnutt, then, is that racism and the drawing of the color line interfere with the market. If you're forced to ride with the malodorous farm laborers because you're poor, that's unfortunate but not unfair. If you're forced to ride with them because you're black, that's another story. So the poor are not victims of discrimination; they are the unfortunate by-products of an essentially just mechanism—the market. Poverty, in other words, is not a civil rights issue. The government kept black people from voting, and eventually the government made it possible for black people to start voting. The government kept women from voting, and it eventually allowed them to vote too. But you don't need the government to keep poor people from shopping at the rich people's mall. And you can't get the government to enable poor people to start shopping there.

The exemplary instance of victimization in modern American political life remains the victim of discrimination. It's the violation of people's rights as citizens—the failure of the liberal state to live up to its liberalism—that we prefer to deplore. The problem in Chesnutt is not that the farm laborers can't afford to ride in the clean comfortable car; it's that some people who can afford to (like Dr. Miller) aren't allowed to. And Leo Frank—"the Jew they lynched in Georgia because of that little factory girl"—is Roth's version of Dr. Miller, a man whose class can't save him from his race. Indeed, part of the attraction of the Leo Frank story may be the way in which it testifies to the triumph of racial prejudice over class privilege, which is to say, the way in which it demonstrates the irrelevance of wealth and (from the standpoint of the racist) turns class warfare into white supremacism while (from the standpoint of the antiracist) turning class warfare into bigotry. If you're a racist, it shows you that racism is the solution; if you're an antiracist, it shows you that racism is the problem. Either way, Tom Watson's anti-Semitism is a kind of gift since it makes over the rational anger of the poor as the irrational anger of the racist and enables everyone to agree that the real issue here is not money but race. So if racism makes economic issues irrelevant by asserting that what really matters is the difference between races, antiracism does exactly the same thing. The difference is just that Chesnutt and Roth condemn what Dixon celebrates. For Roth and Chesnutt, as for Dixon, the fundamental conflicts are between races; antiracism, just as reliably as racism, turns the hostility between rich and poor into the hostility between black and white, Christian and Jew.

At the same time, however, it's important to see that Roth's antiracism (at the beginning of the twenty-first century) means something different from Chesnutt's (at the beginning of the twentieth century). *The Marrow of Tradition* was written at a moment when public figures were competing with each other to proclaim their racism. Tom Watson ran successfully for the Senate on a rabidly Negrophobic platform, and when he died in office, the person appointed to replace him was Rebecca Felton, who became the first woman to serve in that body, and who had brought herself to public attention some twenty-five years before not just by opposing "the negro vote" but by passionately defending mob action against what she called "the black fiend": "if it takes lynching to protect woman's dearest possession from drunken, ravening beasts," she famously declared, "then I say lynch a thousand a week."[18] Nobody made such recommendations about American Jews in the period, but the difference between the Chesnutt and the Roth that I want to stress here is not the one between the place of Negrophobia in American life and the place of anti-Semitism, as fundamental as that difference has been. My point here is the more obvious one: that Chesnutt's antiracism was in 1901 a distinctly minority view, whereas Roth's antiracism is what in 2005 the vast majority of us believe, or at least profess to believe.

When, for example, we look today at old photographs of lynchings, we're shocked not only by the events themselves but by the participants' lack of shame, by the way in which they not only seem happy to be photographed but actually look proud of what they're doing. It's one thing, after all, to be racist; almost all of us are prepared to acknowledge that we each have a little bit of racism hidden away somewhere inside. But it's another thing altogether to be proud of one's racism. Which the lynchers were. Indeed, part of the attraction of lynching was precisely its publicness, its status as an expression of the will of the people. Thus although lynching was always against the law (that's what made it lynching) and often disapproved of, lynchers themselves tended to feel not only that they were doing the right thing but also that they were representing the community. They were doing what everyone knew was right, even if the law was on the other side. And there was a great deal of public support for their view; none of the more than two hundred bills condemning lynching managed to get through the U.S. Congress, and it was not until 2005 that the Senate took any action, in the form of an apology for its earlier failure to act.

But the fact that the Senate in the twenty-first century was extremely (indeed, unanimously) happy to apologize for its failures in the twentieth century has its own significance. For one thing, by 2005, lynching had become more a figure of speech than an actual event, describing people who were (or who claimed to be) treated unfairly (e.g., Clarence Thomas) rather than people who were hanged from a tree or burned at the stake. And, for another, even the fictional representations of lynchings had moved out of the mainstream. It's true that the white supremacists in what is probably the most important racist novel of the recent past, Andrew Macdonald's *The Turner Diaries* (1987), are just as proud as and even more ambitious than Dixon's; they lynch not only black rapists but any black men who sleep with white women, and then they lynch the white women too, adorning their corpses with placards that say, I DEFILED MY RACE.[19] But the audience just isn't there. Where *The Clansman* was published by Doubleday and sold at fine bookstores everywhere, *The Turner Diaries* was published by a white supremacist organization called the National Alliance and was (and is) sold mainly at gun shows. That's where Timothy McVeigh got his copy. And if *The Clansman* is best known today as the racist bestseller that inspired an equally racist blockbuster movie, D. W. Griffith's *The Birth of a Nation* (personally endorsed by President Woodrow Wilson), *The Turner Diaries* is best known today as the inspiration for the bombing of the federal building in Oklahoma City. Woodrow Wilson famously took one of the last things in American society left unsegregrated—the federal civil service—and segregated it. His (and Dixon's and Griffith's) racism was central to American life, a fundamental part of what then was mainstream American political thought. Now, a century later, the racism of *The Turner Diaries* and of Timothy McVeigh has been pushed to the margins.

This doesn't mean that there is no racism in America today or that white supremacism or even anti-Semitism has disappeared; unlike *The Clansman*, *The Turner Diaries*, for example, is hysterically anti-Semitic. But that's one of the proofs of its marginality. Americans today who think that the Israeli secret service is carrying out targeted assassinations in the United States or that Judaism is the religion of "parasites"[20] are more likely to be found hiding from the law in Idaho than making the law in Washington, D.C. In our nation's capital, Israel gets a very good press and Judaism is no parasite; it's the cornerstone of the "Judeo-Christian tradition." Indeed, American Judaism has become so intimately connected with American Christianity that writers like Daniel Pipes who worry about the threat of anti-Semitism worry in the same breath about what he calls that "related phenomenon," the threat of "Anti-Christianism."[21] No mainstream American conservative today wastes a breath complaining that Jews are the problem; indeed a great number of the mainstream conservatives are themselves Jewish.

And even the much more virulent presence of antiblack racism no longer has any public or political purchase. The last Klansman to make a serious run at a serious office was David Duke when in 1991 he ran for governor of Louisiana. And even he, appearing as a guest on *Nightline*, found himself telling Ted Koppel that what he *really* objected to was "racial discrimination," a claim that was hard to believe but significant nonetheless since it suggested how completely racism has been marginalized.[22] Dixon's Clansmen, not to mention Tom Watson and Rebecca Felton, weren't against racial discrimination. Nowadays, as the unfrocked Senate majority leader Trent Lott lives to remind us, politicians are more likely to apologize for their racist remarks than they are to turn them into planks of their campaign platforms. Thus, where *The Marrow of Tradition* was, in its time, a critical and commercial failure, *The Plot Against America* has been just the opposite. And the world that has welcomed Roth's attack on anti-Semitism has become at least equally welcoming of Chesnutt's anti-Negrophobia. If no one wanted to read *The Marrow of Tradition* at the time it was written, lots of people read it now; no doubt every university in the country has at least three or four courses a year in which it gets assigned.

Outside the classroom too, universities are like research and development laboratories for producing new ways to insist that discrimination (as opposed, say, to exploitation) is our fundamental problem. Nothing is more characteristic in this regard than that relatively new phenomenon the antihate rally, which appears to have gotten started in the 1980s but had definitely hit full stride by 1990 (when the then president of Dartmouth,

James Freedman, sponsored one), and is now a regular (sometimes annual, when it takes place during antihate week) event both on and off college campuses. Antihate rallies are obviously different from other kinds of events, such as antiwar rallies; there could be and sometimes are pro-war rallies, but there aren't any pro-hate rallies. Even people who do, in fact, hate don't think it's appropriate to have rallies supporting hate, any more than people who steal things think it's appropriate to have rallies supporting theft. The antihate demonstration, then, is mobilized not in response to the pro-hate position but in response to the expression of what the FBI, in its definition of hate crimes, calls bias. There are a lot of antihate rallies in reaction against people using racial slurs or painting swastikas on dorm walls, and everyone will agree that racial slurs and swastikas on dorm walls are a bad thing. Indeed, it's precisely everyone's agreement that makes antihate rallies so powerful; they express a consensus. But it's also everyone's agreement that makes them a little puzzling. Why are we so committed to combating a position that no one actually holds?

Why, in a world where most of us are not racist (where, on the humanities faculties at our universities, we might more plausibly say not that racism is rare but that it is extinct), do we take so much pleasure in reading attacks on racism? Why do we like it so much that not only do we read books that attack a racism that *no longer* exists (*Plessy* was overruled a half century ago, and it's been a long time since Wilson was president), but we also make bestsellers out of books that attack a racism that *never* existed (Lindbergh never was president). What—to put the question in its most general form—is the meaning of antiracism today?

One way to begin to answer this question might be to suggest that antiracism activates a certain nostalgia. Kenneth Warren's remarks on the recent nostalgia for Jim Crow among some black intellectuals are helpful here. What they're nostalgic for, according to Warren, is black culture. They're nostalgic, in other words, not exactly for racism but for the distinctive social practices (what Cornel West calls the "cultural armor")[23] that the resistance to racism helped create. On the one hand, Jim Crow impoverished and disempowered an entire community; on the other, it solidified that community's identity *as* a community. The creation of a distinctive African American culture was thus both a consequence of racism and a kind of compensation for it. But the meaning of what Warren calls the "cultural turn" in African American political life begins to look very different when the terms of the inequality that produced it begin to change, and this produces a certain awkwardness, especially for successful black intellectuals. Chesnutt's Dr. Miller looks problematic because he doesn't want to ride Jim Crow with the other black people. But he has to. He can't get people to recognize that his class is more important than his race. Today's Dr. Millers look problematic because even when they're riding in what amounts to their very own superdeluxe coach, they think of themselves and want to be thought of by others as riding Jim Crow. They want their race to matter more than their class. And they are nostalgic for Jim Crow because racial segregation created a genuine bond between them and other (poorer, much poorer) black people while the end of segregation placed them in an attractive but difficult position, making possible their great success but only by threatening the bond.[24] Dr. Miller thought that belonging to the black race was not enough to establish community between people of very different classes; the black intellectuals Warren describes hope that belonging to black culture is.

But antiracism serves another more important and more properly political purpose. As we've seen, the central debates about race in America today are no longer debates between racism and antiracism. Rather, the debate today is between two kinds of antiracism. One, identified with multiculturalism and the left, urges us to respect and preserve the differences between blacks and whites and Native Americans and Jews and whoever. It gives poor people identities and, turning them into black people or Latinos or women, insists on regarding their problems as effects of discrimination and intolerance. The other, identified with the right, regards the respect for racial difference as itself a form of discrimination and insists that the only identity that matters (the one we should be respecting) is "American identity." "We are just one race here," as Justice Antonin Scalia put it. "It is American."[25] Where contemporary liberalism's antiracism argues that we can solve our problems by respecting racial difference, contemporary conservatism's antiracism maintains we can solve our problems only by eliminating or ignoring it.

The problem with this debate (or, looked at another way, the virtue of this debate) is that, from the standpoint of economic inequality, it doesn't matter which side you're on and it doesn't matter who wins. Either way, economic inequality is absolutely untouched. The dream of a world free of prejudice, the dream of a world where identities (whether American or hyphenated American) are not discriminated against, is as foundational to the right as it is to the left. And this dream is completely compatible with (is, actually, essential to) the dream of a truly free and efficient market. Here's where the concept of neoliberalism—the idea of the free market as the essential mechanism of social justice—is genuinely clarifying. A society free not only of racism but of sexism and of heterosexism is a neoliberal utopia where all the irrelevant grounds for inequality (your identity) have been eliminated and whatever inequalities are left are therefore legitimated. Thus, when it comes to antiracism, the left is more like a police force for, than an alternative to, the right. Its commitment to rooting out the residual prejudices that too many of us no doubt continue to harbor deep inside is a tacit commitment to the efficiency of the market. And its commitment to the idea that the victims of social injustice today are the victims of racism, sexism and heterosexism (the victims of discrimination rather than exploitation, of intolerance rather than oppression, or of oppression in the form of intolerance) is a commitment to the essential justice of the market. The preferred crimes of neoliberalism are always hate crimes; when our favorite victims are the victims of prejudice, we are all neoliberals.

The U.S. Holocaust Memorial Museum opened in 1993; the National Museum of the American Indian opened on the Mall in 2004 and if Khalid Muhammad had only lived a little longer, he might have died happy since the Board of Regents of the Smithsonian Institution has now approved plans for a National Museum of African-American History and Culture near the Washington Monument. Old-style racists like Jesse Helms were against it, but new-style antiracists like Dick

Cheney and John Roberts and Bill Frist and Thad Cochran (the senator from Mississippi who doesn't make racist remarks) are all for it. It goes without saying, however, that there won't—and that there shouldn't—be a National Museum of Lower-Income Americans on the Mall. It's hard to see what good it would be to poor people to start celebrating their culture, much less their survival as a group. We don't worry that poor people run the risk of assimilation to wealth, which is to say, we don't seek to preserve the distinctive things—the bad educations, the inadequate health care—that make poor people who they are. We do think of at least some poor people as inheriting their poverty, but we don't think of their poverty as their heritage; so, for example, where it makes sense to say of some people that they are "part Jewish" or "part black," we don't think it makes sense to say of anyone that he or she is "part poor" or "part rich." There may be people of mixed race, but there are no people of mixed income; we don't even have the concept of mixed income. Above all, we don't, whether or not we are ourselves poor, think that poverty is just as good as wealth, even if—especially if—we think that poor people are just as good as rich people.

The meaning of antiracism today is thus that it gives us an ideal—the ideal of a society without prejudice—that we can all sign on to at the very moment when the inadequacy of that ideal should be entirely obvious. The gap between the rich and the poor may be growing on a daily basis, but when it comes to difference, we prefer fighting racism to fighting poverty.[26] And the distinction between our conservatives and our liberals is just that our conservatives think we've already won that fight while our liberals think we've only just begun.

Another way to put this is to say that our conservatives and our liberals more or less agree about what a just society would be. That's why mainstream commentators like David Brooks can confidently insist that even though the country seems to be "polarized," "this isn't an ideological moment, liberal or conservative."[27] Of course, no moment ever seems like an ideological moment to Brooks, but he's not alone in this and he's not mistaken. The quarrel between people who think we don't have enough diversity and people who think we have just the right amount is a quarrel over management techniques, not over political ideology. With respect to economic inequality, there is no quarrel; what we might call the neoliberal consensus prevails. The only inequalities we're prepared to do anything about are the ones that interfere with the free market. Chesnutt, insisting that segregation (and especially the law against miscegenation) violated "liberty of contract," was an early adopter. There was no injustice, he thought, in the fact that many people couldn't afford to ride in the first-class car on the train; the injustice was to the people who could afford to ride in that car but weren't allowed to. The injustice was intolerance of racial difference, not acceptance of economic difference.

And this scenario is what gives the fantasy of the rich people's mall its force. The fantasy part, of course, is not that there are such things as rich people's malls. The fantasy is the idea that the injustice in not being able to shop there is the injustice of being discriminated against. Or, to turn the point around, that rich people's malls are fine as long as they're diverse, as long as the black and brown rich people get to buy expensive stuff alongside the white ones. How else can we explain the flurry of disapproval surrounding Hermès's refusal to unlock its doors for some after-hours shopping by Oprah Winfrey? "After-hours shopping is a favor," noted the *Washington Post.* "There's nothing wrong with a store saying not tonight, madame, as long as the reason doesn't have anything to do with skin color."[28] In this universe, social justice means that Oprah Winfrey (like Dr. Miller) ought to be able to spend her money in the same ways the white celebrities (or white doctors) do.

"The problem of the 20th century," W E. B. Du Bois observed at its beginning, will be "the problem of the color line." It looks like the twenty-first century will also be fond of that problem. The difference is that the work that used to be done by racism—the work of obscuring class difference—is now done by antiracism. The ongoing controversy over the government's response to the catastrophe of Hurricane Katrina is, as we noted in the introduction, a case in point. It's like an inverted version of the question about the "rich Jew" Leo Frank: was he lynched because he was Jewish or because he was rich? Is the relevant thing about all those people abandoned in New Orleans the fact that they are black or the fact that they are poor? We like blaming racism, but the truth is there weren't too many rich black people left behind when everybody who could get out of New Orleans did so. The Republican party policies that left the poor behind were not racist, and the economic inequality in American society has grown under Democratic presidents as well as Republicans. This doesn't mean, of course, that racism didn't play a role in New Orleans. It just means that in a society without any racial discrimination, there would still have been poor people who couldn't find their way out of New Orleans. Whereas in a society without poor people (even a racist society without poor people), there wouldn't have been.

3

Richer, Not Better

Here's another name for rich people's malls—universities—although the university where I have taught for the last five years, the University of Illinois at Chicago, is at best a precariously balanced example. UIC is a large and increasingly underfunded public university. Our classrooms are overcrowded. Our physical plant is deteriorating. One of the reasons they hired me was to help raise the ranking of our English Department. But now we can't afford to make any new appointments, so our ambition to make ourselves into a top ten graduate program has become irrelevant. In the midst of all these troubles, however, there is at least one bright spot, one area where we have done well and are poised to do even better. As almost every piece of literature that UIC distributes about itself announces, we are ranked among the top ten universities in the country for the diversity of our student body. And that diversity, the literature goes on to point out, "is one of the greatest aspects of our campus." The bad news about our current condition is that you may be jammed into a classroom so full that you can't find a place to sit. But the good news is that 45 percent of the people jammed in there with you will be Caucasian, 21 percent of them will be Asian, 13 percent of them will be Hispanic and 9 percent will be African American.

It's worth noting that by far our largest minority is Asian American, and that's true of fourteen out of the top twenty in the 2006 *U.S. News and World Report*'s diversity rankings for universities. It's also true that African Americans continue to be underrepresented; Malcolm X would not have been surprised by these figures. But perhaps more notable than the particular numbers in each category are the categories themselves. Although no remark is more common in American public life than the observation that we don't like to talk about race, no remark—as our self-description and the very existence of these rankings suggest—is more false. The eagerness of UIC and every other university to produce its own version of these numbers makes it obvious that, in fact, we love to talk about race. And, in the university, not only do we talk about it; we write books and articles about it, we teach and take classes about it and we arrange our admissions policies in order to take it into account.

We don't, however, so much like to call it race. Indeed, my students, like their teachers, are uncomfortable with the idea of race and prefer to describe the biological differences they see in their classmates as cultural differences. Or, rather, they describe some of the biological differences they see as cultural differences; variations in height and weight don't get the same play variations in skin color do. And, unimpressed by the objection that, speaking the same language, wearing the same clothes, reading the same books, they all seem to me to belong to the same culture, they enthusiastically reproduce not only the official UIC version of their diversity but the official UIC pride in it. They are proud of what they identify as their own cultures and respectful of what they identify as the different cultures of their classmates. Some students might be taller than others, some might be smarter, some might be better looking, but all belong to cultures and all the cultures are worthy of respect.

Needless to say, this is not the way that American universities have always treated racial difference. The function of race in a racist society (like Nazi Germany or Jim Crow America) was precisely to designate some people as more worthy of respect than others, and for many years, as we all know, American universities tried to keep the wrong races out. Today, however, we're trying to get all the races in, and this shift makes sense only in a society that, as we have seen, understands itself not as racist but as antiracist.

It's not, as we noted in the previous chapter, that we have eliminated racism. On the contrary, a remark made almost as often as the one that we don't like to talk about race is the observation that we are all in some way racist, and this one has the merit of being a lot more plausible. But even when *we* are racist, the society to which we are committed is not. This is partly because racism has been pushed to the fringes of public life and partly because racism has been privatized, converted from a political position into a personal failing. The racism that used to be unapologetically public has turned into the very thing that we most often find people publicly apologizing for. Indeed, one of the ways in which the antiracist society functions is precisely through its commitment to eliminating or, at the very least, policing racism. Hence the uproar over the occasional Trent Lott or Rush Limbaugh or Gregg Easterbrook; they remind us that racism is not dead, and they alert us to the necessity of continued vigilance. But this negative police function—as energetically as it's pursued—would be no more than the political correctness it's often accused of being if it weren't accompanied by (in fact, deployed in the service of) a more positive antiracist program.

Racism requires a commitment to the inequality of the races; antiracism requires a commitment to their equality. And here obviously is one key to the attraction of cultural diversity. It gives us a vision of difference without inequality. For our core conception of culture involves the idea that cultures are essentially and in principle equal, and so it makes no sense to think of a society organized into cultures as hierarchical. When we imagine, in other words, that we live in a world divided into different cultures, what we're imagining is that the political commitment to equality involves not creating it (by, say, redistributing wealth) but just insisting that it's already there. The problem, in this account, is that people have for various reasons (e.g., racism) failed to recognize their essential equality; the solution is to get them to recognize it.

The great advantage of culture, then, is that it gives us a model of differences we can love, like those between Asian

Americans and Caucasians rather than differences (like the ones between smart people and stupid people or, more to the point, rich people and poor people) that are not so obviously appealing. And the enthusiasm for the lovable differences is widespread. During my first year at UIC, I happened to give a lecture to an audience of several hundred literature students at Harvard University. This group also prided itself on its diversity, and it was in fact diverse, which is to say, it was a bunch of twenty-year-old kids who were phenotypically different roughly in proportion to the American population (with the usual above-noted exception of the overrepresentation of Asian Americans) and who dressed a little less differently than they looked but who really did like different kinds of music. What they had in common was nothing but their very high SAT scores and, not coincidentally, their wealth—a fact that the satisfaction they took in their diversity rendered at best (to them) uninteresting and at worst irrelevant. When asked about the differences between them as a group and a parallel group of literature students at UIC, they were prepared to acknowledge that the UIC students might be even more diverse than they are (remember, UIC's ranked in the top ten; Harvard's only ranked fortieth), but they were unable to see any significance in the fact that the UIC group was less wealthy. This is equally true of the students at UIC, who identify themselves as black, white, Arab, Asian, Hispanic, whatever, but not as middle- or working-class. After all, your ethnicity is something you can be proud of in a way that your poverty or even your wealth (since it's your parents' wealth) is not.

But the greatest value of diversity is not primarily in the

contribution it makes to students' self-esteem. Its real value, as the widespread acceptance of affirmative action shows, is in the contribution it makes to the collective fantasy that institutions like Harvard and UIC are—internally and in relation to each other—meritocracies. For if the students at Harvard are appropriately diverse, we know that no student is being kept from Harvard because of his or her race or culture. Every institution, in an ideal affirmative-action world, has the right cultural mix. How, then, do some students end up at Harvard and some at UIC? Since the differences between them that produce this divergence are not (indeed cannot be) cultural (remember, cultures are equal), they are attributed instead to the merit of the individual. As long as we think of people as belonging to cultures and we think of cultures as equal, we are enabled also to think of the inequalities between people (their test scores, for example) as individual.

This helps explain the popularity on campus (especially among students at the most elite campuses) of affirmative action; it is a powerful tool for legitimizing their sense of their individual merit. Affirmative action guarantees that all cultures will be represented on campus, that no one will be penalized unjustly for belonging to a culture, and therefore that the white students on campus can understand themselves to be there on merit because they didn't get there at the expense of any black people. The problem with affirmative action is not (as is often said) that it violates the principles of meritocracy; the problem is that it produces the illusion that we actually *have* a meritocracy. We are often reminded of how white our classrooms would look if we did away with affirmative action. But imagine what that Harvard classroom would look like if instead we replaced race-based affirmative action with a genuinely class-based affirmative action. The median family income in the United States today is a little over $54,000 per year;[1] almost 90 percent of Harvard students come from families with more than that, so at least half of them would have to go. And almost 75 percent of Harvard students come from families with incomes over $100,000 per year, although only a little over 20 percent of American families have incomes that high. So most of them would have to go too. If the income distribution at Harvard were made to look like the income distribution of the United States, over half the people in that room would be gone and a great many of the disappeared would be rich and white. It's no wonder that rich white kids and their parents aren't complaining about diversity. Race-based affirmative action, from this standpoint, is a kind of collective bribe rich people pay themselves for ignoring economic inequality. The fact (and it is a fact) that it doesn't help to be white to get into Harvard replaces the much more fundamental fact that it does help to be rich and that it's virtually essential not to be poor.

Hence the irrelevance of Harvard's 2004 announcement that it wouldn't ask parents who earn less than $40,000 a year to help pay for their children's education, an irrelevance that has only been increased by the fact that it has already (starting in 2006) raised the income ceiling to $60,000.[2] While this is no doubt great news to those financially pressed students who have gone to top high schools, taken college-prep courses and scored well on their SATs, it's bound to seem a little beside the point to the great majority of the poor, since what's keeping them out of elite universities is not their inability to pay the bill but their inability to qualify for admission in the first place. Even if elite schools followed what is meant to be the radical advice of the *Los Angeles Times*'s Peter Hong, who urges Harvard to send an "even more powerful message" by eliminating tuition altogether, it wouldn't be of much use to the poor, since by far the largest beneficiaries would be the rich and upper-middle-class students whose parents have paid for private schools or bought houses in expensive neighborhoods, thereby subsidizing the best public schools with their property taxes.[3] Finally, after spending all that money (private schools in New York can now run over $30,000 a year; the "platinum package" at a "college preparation service" like IvyWise costs another $30,000;[4] the houses in the really good suburbs cost millions), they would catch a break—free Harvard!

Harvard is not likely to eliminate tuition, but the major trend in American education certainly has been toward rewarding the wealthy when it comes time to pay for college. This is obvious at public universities, where the number of students coming from rich families has risen sharply in the last few years. At schools like the University of Michigan and the University of Illinois at Urbana-Champaign, 40 percent of the freshmen in 2004 came from families making over $100,000 a year.[5] And it's even more obvious with respect to the widespread replacement of need-based with merit-based scholarships. Donald Heller and Christopher Rasmussen make this point sharply in their assessment of the effect of the Michigan Merit Award Scholarship Program, funded by tobacco lawsuit settlement funds and designed "to increase access to post-secondary education."[6] They show that at a school like Grosse Ile High, where 64 percent of the students qualified for the merit scholarships, 94 percent of the graduating seniors were already heading to college before the program was established. At Hamtramck High School, by contrast, the college participation rate is only 30 percent and only 14 percent of the students qualified for the award. So these scholarships don't increase access to college; they mainly provide extra funds for kids who were already going. Furthermore, the kids who are already going are the ones who least need the scholarships in the first place. The median family income in Grosse Ile is $96,226 a year. The median family income in Hamtramck is $30,496 a year. One way you can put it is that where need-based scholarships give money to the poor, merit-based scholarships give money to the deserving. Another way you can put it is that where need-based scholarships give money to the poor, merit-based scholarships give money to the rich.[7]

In this respect, the concept of affirmative action is potentially useful after all. We can just think of need-based scholarships as a kind of affirmative action for the poor, and there is some evidence that, especially where race-based admissions have been banned (e.g., Texas and California), there have been new efforts to make universities more diverse by giving admissions points for things like "low family income." But if cultural diversity is the goal of race-based affirmative action, it's hard to see how economic diversity can work the same way. It's hard to see, that is, how the justification that it's good for the white kids to get to know a few black kids can be translated into the justification that it's good for the rich kids to get to know a few poor ones. And the kind of diversity produced by a larger number of poor students isn't exactly the sort of thing a college can plausibly celebrate—no poor people's history month, no special "theme" dormitories (i.e., no Poor House alongside Latino House and Asia House) and no special reunions for poor alumni. Indeed, the whole point of going to Harvard, from the standpoint of the poor, would be to stop being poor, whereas Asian Americans, African Americans, Latinos, et cetera, presumably don't want to stop being Asian American, African American, et cetera. What justifies affirmative action for poor people is that it has nothing to do with diversity; it's supposed to help poor people go to college *despite* the fact that they're poor. And what makes the notion of economic diversity look ridiculous is also what makes it so attractive: it reassures us that the problem of poverty is like the problem of race and that the way to solve it is by appreciating rather than minimizing our differences.

We like diversity and we like programs such as affirmative action because they tell us that racism is the problem we need to solve and that solving it requires us just to give up our prejudices. (Solving the problem of economic inequality might require something more; it might require us to give up our money.) This attitude helps to account for the continuing popularity of racism as a target of student activism and the more general phenomenon of the "antihate" rally as a mobilizing force. As long as the presumed object of our hatred is difference, everyone (we're all a little racist or a little homophobic) can feel responsible for the problem and proud of their contribution to the solution. "It's our fault, it's all our faults," the *Chicago Tribune* quoted a Northwestern University student, talking about a recent flurry of racist and homophobic incidents on campus. And even when the incidents turned out to be mainly hoaxes, members of the university community were able to take some satisfaction in the various "antihate" activities they generated. "Positive things are coming out of this," observed the director of the Hillel Center on campus, since the incidents (even if staged) "have galvanized students to think about how to be more proactive in their activities and their friendships to make sure all students on campus feel comfortable here."[8] It's not, of course, surprising that universities like Northwestern should want their students to feel "comfortable" or that, given the nearly $40,000 a year it's costing their families to send them there, the students should expect comfort.

It's also not surprising that the graduates of universities like Northwestern should expect to have their comfort levels maintained at the next stage of their careers. When a few months after the Northwestern incidents, an e-mail went the rounds of the law firm of Dewey Ballantine, urging the owner of some puppies being offered for adoption not to "let them go to a Chinese restaurant," the *New York Times* headline read "Asian-Americans Take Offense" and the story quoted the co-chairwoman of the Asian Pacific Law Students Association as wanting to know: "What is going to change this environment? What is going to make it easier? What is going to make Asian-Americans comfortable about going back to Dewey?"[9] It makes sense that upper-middle-class lawyers would expect to have their employer be as solicitous of their comfort as their university was and that their expectations would be fulfilled. Why shouldn't Dewey Ballantine be at least as eager as Northwestern to make things easier for a workforce that is not only well remunerated (starting salary for an associate is $125,000 a year) but highly remunerative (revenue per lawyer is $780,000 a year)?[10]

What *is* surprising is that the politics of diversity—which is to say, the goal of making students and lawyers more "comfortable"—should have emerged as the hallmark of liberalism. The right-wing position here is that discrimination is mainly a thing of the past, that these people are much too sensitive; the upper middle class is perfectly comfortable. The left-wing position is that racism and discrimination are very much alive; the upper middle class isn't comfortable enough. Identified with the commitment to diversity, left-wing politics is here transformed into a code of manners, a way of talking and acting designed not to produce radical social change but to ensure instead that no one is offended. And, in fact, the left and the right can collaborate in what has become a new commitment not only to making people comfortable with their difference but to making them feel better about their inferiority.

◆

Indeed, when it comes to making poor people feel better, proudly antiliberal writers like—President George W. Bush's favorite—Tom Wolfe are at the cutting edge. Where the Philip Roths and Toni Morrisons continue to be outraged by racism, the heroine of Wolfe's most recent novel, *I Am Charlotte Simmons*, is the kind of person more likely to bring suit against affirmative action than to benefit from it. Like the heroine of another recent effort to think about class, Lee in Curtis Sittenfeld's *Prep*, Wolfe's Charlotte Simmons is a poor *white* girl, and the social troubles both she and Lee experience have nothing to do with Negrophobia or anti-Semitism. The scariest thing about the first day of school for these girls is finding out what the other girls are wearing (the answer at both schools is flip-flops and shorts), and the hardest thing is surviving the moment when your family meets your new roommate's family. Charlotte is relieved when she sees the flip-flops and the shorts, since she's wearing shorts too; Sittenfeld's Lee is horrified, because she's wearing "a long dress with peach and lavender flowers and a lace collar."[11] But Charlotte's advantage disappears when it comes to the families since, although Lee is "embarrassed" by her father, Charlotte is "mortified" by hers. What embarrasses Lee is that her father responds, "No sir, I'm in the mattress business" to her roommate's father, who, having heard they're from South Bend, says, "I take it you teach at Notre Dame." "I was embarrassed that my father called Dede's father sir," Lee says, "embarrassed by his job, and embarrassed by our rusted white Datsun." Charlotte's mortification trumps Lee's embarrassment on every count, from the car (since her daddy drives a rusted-out pickup truck with a fiberglass camper top) to the job (he doesn't actually have one): "Used to be I operated a last-cutting machine over't the Thorn McAn factory in Sparta, but Thorn McAn, they relocated to Mexico." Now "I take care—keer—of a house some summer people got over't Roaring Gap."[12]

So Charlotte is at her college (reputedly modeled on Duke)

on a scholarship, and Lee is also on scholarship at her prep school (modeled on Groton, where Sittenfeld herself went, and where Charlotte's roommate is supposed to have gone). And the meaning of all the embarrassment is more social than personal. Anybody can be embarrassed by her parents, but these girls are embarrassed by their parents' class, by the fact that (at Groton and Duke if not in the world), everybody else is rich, or at least, richer. Charlotte's daddy even produces a few rueful complaints about globalization for the edification of the roommate's CEO dad until he remembers his manners and apologizes for talking politics at the dinner table. But the point is made. "American writers," Lionel Trilling wrote in *The Liberal Imagination*, "have a kind of resistance to looking closely at society," and by *society* he meant "class" and, in particular, "the meeting and conflict of diverse social classes."[13] Of course, it was "American writers of genius" (Faulkner, Dos Passos, etc.) that Trilling was interested in, and while the verdict is still out on the thirty-something Curtis Sittenfeld, it's pretty clear that the seventy-something Tom Wolfe hasn't made it. But they do get credit for attempting to imagine an America in which the fact that some people have more money than others matters. Reading Philip Roth, you'd think the big issue in American life was anti-Semitism. Which is not that far from what you'd think reading recent novels by Jonathan Safran Foer and Michael Chabon.

The downside of globalization, however, is not Wolfe's central preoccupation. He is, after all, President Bush's favorite novelist, and he tells every interviewer who will talk to him how much he enjoys taunting the out-of-touch "liberal elite" at dinner parties with his own support for the president. (They react, he says, as if he'd announced he was a child molester.) So what makes college life hard for Charlotte isn't her poverty; it's her *Shamela*-like "vartue" and her intellectual seriousness. Where all the other kids want to get drunk and hook up, Charlotte just wants to read the *Annals of Cognitive Biology* and *Madame Bovary* "in French." But even that isn't the real problem; what drives Charlotte and Wolfe crazy is not the anti-intellectualism or the promiscuity (which, in fact, he describes with a kind of creepy enthusiasm that makes the child molester thing hit a little too close to home). It's the "condescension"; it's the way all the students who went to Groton and whose parents never got laid off by Thom McAn and who know exactly what to wear and what attitudes to have—"the liberal elite"—make Charlotte feel as if they are better than she is. The equivalent in *Prep* is being identified as "LMC" (lower middle class), although, because Sittenfeld's Lee is not herself immune to its attractions, *Prep* has a more interesting relation to elitism than *Charlotte Simmons* does. Charlotte despises a world in which anybody is judged as LMC; Lee doesn't like the world in which *she* is judged as LMC; being LMC is what she went to prep school to escape.

Both these novels understand themselves, then, as concerned with class privilege, and *Prep* even ends with Lee being interviewed by the *Times* and getting into trouble with her teachers and her classmates when the interview is published because she told the reporter that the difference between the rich and the poor is visible in "the quality of their stuff" and in the fact that some people send their laundry "to a service" while others do it themselves "in the dorm machines."[14] Hence the "condescension" problem, the suggestion that what's wrong with elite institutions is the way they make poor people feel their poverty. And hence the solution: poor people shouldn't be made to feel inferior, either in novels or in life. Thus, in a recent real-world application, the *Harvard Crimson* is unhappy about Dormaid, a new service that offers to clean students' rooms for eighty-five dollars. The "obvious display of wealth," the *Crimson* objects (neither Charlotte nor Lee could afford Dormaid), "will establish a perceived, if unspoken, barrier between students of different economic means" and thus compromise the "egalitarian nature of dorm life." "There are both rich people and poor people at Harvard," the *Crimson* tells us (and so do *Prep* and *I Am Charlotte Simmons*); keeping maids out of the dorms will eliminate what the *Crimson* brilliantly calls the "unneeded distinctions between the rich and the poor."[15]

But, as we've already seen, it's not really true that there are rich people and poor people at Harvard. There are very few poor people at Harvard or, for that matter, at any of the 146 colleges that count as "selective": 3 percent of the students in these institutions come from where Charlotte Simmons is supposed to come from, the lowest socioeconomic quarter of American society; 74 percent come from the highest. As Richard D. Kahlenberg puts it, you are "twenty-five times as likely to run into a rich student as a poor student" at schools like Harvard and Duke.[16] And from this perspective, we can see that the point of objecting to conspicuous displays of wealth at school is not so much to avoid offending the poor people at

Harvard as it is to pretend that there are poor people at Harvard to be offended. Indeed, that's what the attraction of the scholarship novel is itself all about; the work it does is not in exposing the injustices of class difference at Groton and Duke but in pretending that there *are* class differences at Groton and Duke. If Trilling thought that major American writers were unwilling to write about the class differences that were staring them in the face in 1947,[17] minor American writers in 2005 are so eager to write about class difference that they describe it even where it doesn't actually exist.

Which is not to say that there is less class difference in 2005 than there was when Trilling was writing. Just the opposite. As it happens, the U.S. Census begins its "Historical Income Tables" in 1947; in that year (figured in constant 2004 dollars), the difference between the annual income of those in the twentieth percentile of the American population and those in the eightieth percentile was a little under $24,000. In 2005, that difference was over $75,000. It's not difficult, in other words, to understand why class difference might have been hard to see in 1947—there wasn't nearly as much of it. And it's not so difficult to understand why we try to make it visible today in places like elite schools where there's still, albeit for very different reasons, very little of it. For as economic inequality has increased, we have become increasingly committed to imagining that our schools are open to all, regardless of class. In 1947, everyone knew that Ivy League colleges were mainly for the children of the rich, but no one much cared. Today, however, we've all begun to care, so it's important that we don't really know.

Schools loom larger in the neoliberal imagination than they did in the liberal imagination because schools have become our primary mechanism for convincing ourselves that poor people deserve their poverty. Or, to put the point the other way around, schools have become our primary mechanism for convincing rich people that they deserve their wealth. Everybody understands that people who go to elite schools have a sizable economic advantage over people who don't; that's one reason people want to go to them.[18] And as long as the elite schools are themselves open to anybody who's smart enough and/or hardworking enough to get into them, we see no injustice in reaping the benefits. It's OK if schools are technologies for producing inequality as long as they are also technologies for justifying it. But the justification will only work if, as the *Crimson* hopefully asserts, there really are rich people and poor people at Harvard. If there really aren't; if it's your wealth (or your family's wealth) that makes it possible for you to go the elite school in the first place, then, of course, the real source of your success is not the fact that you went to an elite school but the fact that your parents were rich enough to give you the kind of background and preparation that got you admitted to the elite school.

SAT scores continue to be a state-of-the-art example. The justification of the SAT is its correlation with (and hence its function as a predictor of) college grades. The other thing it correlates with—"about as well as with college grades," as Nicholas Lemann puts it[19]—is family income. So if you look at a chart mapping family income with SAT scores, the numbers rise in tandem, like this:

ANNUAL FAMILY INCOME	AVERAGE SAT SCORE		
	Verbal	*Math*	*Total*
Less than $10,000	422	450	872
$10,000–$20,000	440	457	887
$20,000–$30,000	459	467	926
$30,000–$40,000	478	482	960
$40,000–$50,000	493	496	989
$50,000–$60,000	501	504	1005
$60,000–$70,000	507	510	1017
$70,000–$80,000	515	518	1033
$80,000–$100,000	527	530	1057
More than $100,000	553	562	1115

SOURCE: College Board, *College-Bound Seniors 2004: A Profile of SAT Program Test Takers*

It's probably not true, however, that family *income* alone is the most reliable financial indicator of success in education. Blacks, for example, tend to do less well than whites in many areas of educational performance even when their family incomes are the same. (And, of course, this has led the *Bell Curve* types to propose racial difference as the explanation.) But the sociologist Dalton Conley argues that if you replace family income by family wealth—if, in other words, you take what he calls "accumulated wealth" (in the form of assets like stocks, bonds, savings accounts and home equity) as well as family income into account when measuring a family's economic status—the gap between blacks and whites disappears. And this is true not only in educational attainment. One of Conley's most striking findings is that the single best predictor of the net worth of the people he studied was not their race or even their income but the net worth of their parents. More generally, he argues, supposedly "tenacious racial differences" (like high school and college graduation rates) are really the effects of "class differences."[20]

So on the one hand, we get affirmative action in universities, which solves a problem that no longer exists. It's their lack of family wealth, not the color of their skin, that disproportionately keeps blacks out of elite colleges. And on the other hand, we get the ban on Dormaid, which also solves a problem that doesn't exist. The injury done to the poor by our school system has taken place long before anyone gets to Harvard. But this doesn't mean that these solutions to fake problems serve no purpose. The purpose they serve is to disguise the real problem. We need, as I've already suggested, to believe that poor people aren't kept out of our elite universities in order to also believe that the economic advantages conferred by going to them are earned and so are justified. If going to Harvard is more a reflection of your family's wealth than it is of your merit, if it's a *sign* of privilege rather than a *cause* of it, then, of course, the legitimating effect disappears. So the real point of eliminating the unneeded class differences at Harvard is to conceal the needed ones, the ones that got all the kids from the top quarter into Harvard in the first place. The function of the (very few) poor people at Harvard is to reassure the (very many) rich people at Harvard that you can't just buy your way into Harvard.

Naturally, novels about scholarship students make only a minor contribution to convincing us that the students in elite colleges are there because they deserve to be. Affirmative action—which functions to convince all the white kids that they didn't get in just because they were white—plays a somewhat bigger role. The biggest role of all, however, is played by the intense competition among the rich kids to get into the most prestigious of the elite schools. No moment in *Prep* is more believable than when the bad behavior of a senior is explained by the fact that he's "bitter" "because he's going to Trinity" (a respectable private college in Hartford, Connecticut) instead of to one of his top choices. And this is because you really do have to work hard and be smart (or athletic or talented in some real and distinctive way) to be able to go to a school like Harvard instead of a school like Trinity.

But while it no doubt matters to your self-esteem if you go to one of the really prestigious elite schools instead of to one of the not-so-prestigious ones, it doesn't much matter to your economic position; the graduates of Trinity are also being ushered out of upper-middle-class adolescence into upper-middle-class adulthood. The difference between the people who go to Trinity and the ones who go to Harvard is a difference in status, not class. Status, as Richard Sennett says in *Respect in a World of Inequality*, "usually refers to where a person stands in a social hierarchy," but it's crucially not reducible to where a person stands economically.[21] Rather, the inequalities of status presume a certain equality of wealth. The happy senior who's been admitted to Brown has a higher status than the "bitter" one who's going to Trinity only insofar as whatever economic difference there may be between them doesn't count. Indeed, inequalities of status are never more powerful than when they're utterly disconnected from inequalities of class. If we can't imagine that we competed on a level playing field, how can we take any pleasure in winning?

Because status is not reducible to money, you can think of your high status as having nothing to do with your wealth. And just as the rewards of status presume the irrelevance of material inequality, so do its defeats. When you think your real problem is not that people have more money than you but that the people who have more money condescend to you, your problem is status. And when the solution to your problem is (what Sennett recommends) "mutual respect across the boundaries of inequality" (i.e., no more condescending), you have the imaginative world of neoliberalism, the world where it's OK for a few people to be rich and a lot of people to be poor but where it's definitely not OK to make anyone feel bad about being poor, where it's important above all to remember that there's nothing wrong with being poor and where, as Lee's mom says, "being rich doesn't make you a better person."

The message that there's nothing wrong with being richer than everyone else (hey, you earned it!) as long as you don't *act* like being rich makes you better than everyone else is conveyed not just in novels but at every level of American life, from electoral politics (John Kerry fits right in here) to reality TV. A truly brilliant episode of the otherwise undistinguished show *Wife Swap* makes the point even more effectively than Lee's mom does. The wives who get swapped are rich Jodi (who has not only inherited money but married a man who makes a lot of it) and poor (or at best working-class) Lynn. Where Jodi spends most of her time working out and shopping ("me time"), with an hour or so a day for her kids (the four nannies do the heavy lifting), Lynn drives a schoolbus, chops wood, cleans her run-down house and spends every remaining moment with her kids. What do they learn when they trade lives for a couple of weeks? Rich Jodi learns that she ought to spend more time with her children. (When she goes home, she'll have dinner with them a lot more often.) Poor Lynn learns that she's better off where she is than on the Upper East Side; "Money," she says, "can't buy what I have." And poor Lynn's husband, with no one around to do the housework, learns what a treasure his wife is.

The only one who doesn't learn anything is Jodi's rich husband, Stephen, the villain of the piece, condemned not only by Lynn but by every critic who reviewed the show because he starts and ends the two weeks a "snob." In contrast to his rich spoiled wife, who has realized, she says, that "I have a little bit of prejudice in me against people who come from different worlds and live different lives" (she can't quite bring herself to say "poor people"), Stephen openly "looks down," as Lynn puts it, on poor people at the beginning of the show, and, although he unconvincingly claims "It had nothing to do with finances," he is still looking down on them at the end. He doesn't like Lynn's taste in food, in clothes or in decorating the house. So if the first point of the show is that moms should spend more time with their children, a point that every participant and every critic got (although a few left-behind feminists complained about the unfairness of requiring it to be the mom), the second point—received with unanimous approval—is that the rich shouldn't look down on the poor, that the poor deserve to be treated, as Lynn says, with "respect."

At no time, apparently, did it occur to the makers of the show, the people in it or the people reviewing it, that what the show really demonstrates is how much better it is to be rich than to be poor. Or perhaps one should say not that the show ignores this point but that it is devoted to denying it, and that it succeeds so completely (this is its brilliance) that we find ourselves believing that run-down shacks in the woods are just as nice as Park Avenue apartments, especially if your husband remembers to thank you for chopping the wood when you get home from driving the bus. The idea the show likes is the one Tom Wolfe and company like: that the problem with being poor is not having less money than rich people but having rich people "look down" on you. And the rich husband is bad because he does indeed look down on the poor people, whereas the rich wife (the one who has never done a day's work in her life and who begins the show by celebrating her "me time," shopping, working out, etc.) turns out to be good because she comes to appreciate the poor and even to realize that she can learn from them. The fault here is not in being rich but in thinking that you have better taste—more generally, in thinking that (Lee's mother to the contrary notwithstanding) you *are* a better person.

American egalitarianism—or antielitism—thus takes two contradictory but surprisingly complementary forms. The first consists in thinking not that you're better because you're rich (that would be snobbery) but instead that you got rich because you're better. That's what got you into Harvard! That's what got you all the money! In this form of egalitarianism, we pretend that everybody had an equal chance. The second kind of egalitarianism consists in thinking that it doesn't matter what colleges people go to, that it doesn't matter how much money they have—no one's better than anyone else. Here we insist that there are no advantages to being rich and that people who went to good colleges are in no way superior to people who didn't. And if the contradiction is obvious (I got to go to Harvard because I'm better than you; just because I went to Harvard, that doesn't make me better than you), the complementarity is even more obvious (there's nothing better about being rich; there's nothing worse about being poor).

Or, as David Brooks has put it, "In America," "nobody is better, nobody is worse." Thus his famous comparison of the differences in American life to those in a high school cafeteria, divided into nerds, geeks, jocks, et cetera—they're not classes, they're "cliques."[22] Sure the jocks have a higher status, but they're not really better than the nerds, and just as the jocks shouldn't be boastful, the nerds shouldn't be resentful. The jocks shouldn't be bullies; the nerds shouldn't bring their Kalashnikovs to school.

On this model, then, class is turned into clique, and once the advantages of class are redescribed as the advantages of status, we get the recipe for what we might call right-wing egalitarianism: respect the poor. Which is also, as it turns out, a major ingredient in left-wing egalitarianism. Where the (neoliberal) right likes status instead of class, the (neoliberal) left likes culture, and the diversity version of respect the poor is respect the Other. The Other is different from you and me, but, just as Brooks says, neither better nor worse. That's why multiculturalism could go from proclaiming itself a subversive politics to taking up its position as a corporate management tool (try getting your MBA without taking a course like Managing Diversity or Managing a Multicultural Workforce) in about ten minutes and without having to make the slightest adjustment. Indeed, from this perspective, respecting the Other can't help but be attractive to corporate managers, whatever their politics might be. What CEO doesn't find it easier to respect his employees' culture than to pay them a decent wage?

Cultures, like cliques, give us all the advantages of what Brooks calls "different sensibilities" (rich Jodi calls them "different worlds") without the disadvantages of different incomes. They turn what Trilling called "diverse social classes" into what we just call diversity, and they give us what we might call the fantasy rather than the reality of a left politics, a politics defined by its opposition to racism, sexism and homophobia, and hence by the idea that what we should do with difference is not eliminate it but, like Jodi, learn to appreciate it. So where Trilling, a half century ago, thought "there were no conservative or reactionary ideas in general circulation," it's tempting today to say just the opposite. Indeed, we might more plausibly describe contemporary politics and contemporary political argument as nothing but a dispute between our reactionaries and our conservatives. The reactionaries are the ones who attack diversity, the conservatives are the ones who defend it; the reactionaries are the ones who think our inequalities are justified, the conservatives are the ones who think we don't have any or, more precisely, that the ones we do have are the products of prejudice, of treating people as if they were worse than we are. They think, in other words, that our problem is the *illusion* of inequality, and that if we could just get rid of the illusion (racism, sexism, especially classism), we'd be fine.

Classism is the key here because classism is the pseudo-problem that brings left and right, conservatives and reactionaries together, and it's why otherwise utterly anodyne texts like *Prep* and *I Am Charlotte Simmons* have a certain interest. Classism is what you're a victim of not because you're poor but because people aren't nice to you because you're poor.[23] Its origins are on the left, in the old academic trinity (race, gender, class), and it treats economic difference along the lines of racial and sexual difference, thus identifying the problem not as the difference but as the prejudice (racism, sexism) against the difference. So, just as to be opposed to racism is by no means to be opposed to racial difference, to be opposed to classism is by no means to oppose class difference. And once you're more committed to respecting class difference than to eliminating it, it doesn't much matter whether you still think of yourself as being on the left; the opposition to classism is at least as attractive to the right. When Tom Wolfe makes fun of the liberal elite at New York dinner parties, it's their classism, their sense that they understand politics, art and literature better than, say, Charlotte Simmons's dad, that he's making fun of. Every right-wing Republican who runs against the liberal media or Hollywood is waving the banner of classism, even when he or she has never heard of the word.[24] If left-wing political correctness dictates that we not act as if Western culture is superior to other cultures, right-wing political correctness dictates that we not act as if rich people are superior to poor people.

But, of course, it's not true that the problem with being poor is that people with more money don't think of you as their equal. The problem is that, with respect to money, they're right. And this problem would not be solved if rich people stopped looking down on poor people and started appreciating them instead. For while it may be plausible to think of cultures as different but equal, it cannot be plausible to think of classes in the same way. Defined on a vertical axis—upper, middle, lower—classes are nothing but structures of inequality.[25] Blaming the victim (treating poor people as if they were responsible for their poverty) may be bad, but it's hard to see how congratulating the victim (I love what you've done with your shack!) is better.

There are two points here. The first is that politics has been reduced to nothing but etiquette. But this shouldn't come as much of a surprise. After all, the politics of making everyone comfortable—of respecting difference—never was anything but etiquette. But one would have thought that this was a politics that could not plausibly be extended beyond the victims of discrimination or intolerance, since the problem with being poor, as we've already had occasion to observe, is not the lack of respect but the lack of money. The true victims of the injustice in our educational system are not the students who have been made to feel uncomfortable on the campuses of Duke, Northwestern and Harvard but the ones who have never set foot on these campuses or on any other. What is surprising is that the battles over social justice in the university have taken the form of battles over cultural diversity, which is to say, of battles over what color skin the rich kids should have. If you belong economically to the bottom half of American families (or even to the bottom three quarters), you will not benefit from having your ethnicity respected by the other students at Northwestern, you will not suffer by being made to feel uncomfortable by the partners at Dewey Ballantine. Diversity, like gout, is a rich people's problem. And it is also a rich people's solution, as attractive to rich people on the left as it is (or ought to be) to rich people on the right. For as long as we're committed to thinking of difference as something that should be respected, we don't have to worry about it as something that should be eliminated. As long as we think that our best universities are fair if they are appropriately diverse, we don't have to worry that most people can't go to them and that the people who do get to go to them do so because they've had the good luck to be born into relatively wealthy families. As long, in other words, as the left continues to worry about diversity, the right won't have to worry about inequality.

The second point is that when economic inequality *does* nevertheless manage to rear its ugly head, the left has provided the right a useful technology for learning to love it. Ungrateful conservatives often complain about the political correctness of liberals, but the liberalism that strives to achieve equality by celebrating diversity is a liberalism that every conservative should love and that the opponents of the liberal elite have put to good use. What the commitment to diversity seeks is not a society in which there are no poor people but one in which there's nothing wrong with being poor, a society in which poor people—like blacks and Jews and Asians—are respected. And in the effort to create such a world, liberalism has ended up playing a useful if no doubt unintended role, the role of supplying the right with just the kind of left it wants. What the right wants is culture wars instead of class wars because as long as the wars are about identity instead of money, it doesn't matter who wins. And the left gives it what it wants.

For neoliberals on the left and on the right, in other words, it's prejudice, not poverty, that counts as the problem, and if, at the heart of the liberal imagination, as Trilling understood it, was the desire not to have to think about class difference, at the heart of the neoliberal imagination is the desire not to have to get rid of class difference. Sometimes that desire takes the form of pretending it doesn't exist (no maid service in the dorms); more often it takes the form of pretending it does exist (there are rich students and poor students at Harvard). Almost always it takes the form of insisting that class doesn't matter, or of redefining class so that it looks like culture. Of course it might be objected that, when it comes to being healthier, safer, freer and happier, being rich does indeed make you better and that a more just society would imagine a more just distribution of money, health, safety and freedom. But the politics of the neoliberal imagination involves respecting the poor, not getting rid of poverty—eliminating inequality without redistributing wealth. And until that changes, our best hope for economic egalitarianism would seem to be the recently announced spike in theft on the subways, due, the transit police say, to kids stealing iPods, from, we can hope, the graduates of universities like Duke, which has started giving them away free to Charlotte Simmons and her classmates.

4

Just and Unjust Rewards

The commitment to diversity shouldn't be and hasn't been limited to the phantasms we call races. While it's true that the problem of gender inequality has never reared its ugly head among the shoppers at Hermes and has been pretty much banished from the dormitories of the Ivy League, it remains a live issue in the workplace—from the employees at the poor people's mall (Wal-Mart) to those at the richest of the rich people's universities (Harvard). At Wal-Mart, the issue has been unequal pay for women; a recent lawsuit alleges that women are paid an average of 30 percent less than men. At Harvard, the issue has been that women are underrepresented in at least one area—math and sciences—on the faculty. And what brought the issue to national attention was a set of incendiary remarks by the university's president, Lawrence Summers, suggesting that women might be biologically ill equipped to become scientists and eventually producing not only a series of apologies and retractions (culminating in the president's resignation) but a financial commitment of $50 million to increase diversity at Harvard.

Was this a good result? Was it a step forward for equality at Harvard? Well, if it somehow turns out that President Summers was right in the first place, probably not. It goes without saying there are lots of biological differences between the sexes which certainly make each of them better suited for certain kinds of activities. If, implausibly enough, it turns out that men really are better at math, presumably math departments at universities will always contain more men than women, just as it might turn out that if women (almost equally implausibly) are more articulate than men, law schools may end up containing more women. In fact, the number of women attending American law schools has quadrupled since the 1970s, and they are now almost half the student body.[1] Maybe a hundred years from now almost all the mathematicians will (still) be men and almost all the lawyers and law professors will be women. If those results are produced by something like Summers's fantasy of biological predisposition, it's hard to see why that would be a problem, any more than, say, it's a problem that most professional basketball players are tall and most professional musicians have good ears.

But what if Summers is wrong and the lack of diversity in the Harvard math department is not a function of biology? Why should we care about the diversity of the Harvard faculty? Who are the victims of the lack of diversity? Suppose that neither sex has a biological math advantage. It's just that for socially stereotypical reasons men go disproportionately (are pushed) into math and women (are pushed) into law. Well, here we do have some victims. We have people who are ending up in professions that, absent any social pressure, they might not have chosen. We have lawyers who would rather have been math professors and mathematicians who would rather have been lawyers. But, for reasons that the preceding chapters have already begun to make obvious, it's a little hard to think of this as a crucial issue in American life, one that can plausibly separate liberals (outraged by Summers's initial indifference to diversity) from conservatives (outraged by his eventual capitulation to it). Because, of course, the real victims in the American system of education are not people who feel social pressure to become lawyers instead of mathematicians. When, for example, the physics teacher at the preparatory school run by the University of Chicago tells the *Chicago Tribune* that the "dirty little secret in physics is that there aren't enough women in it—which is like locking up half the talent pool,"[2] he is mistaken. Way more than half the talent pool has been locked up—the huge majority that never sees the inside of a place like the Lab School—and unlocking the women of the upper middle class won't make much of a dent in that. Indeed, although bestowing on the women of the upper middle class all the privileges already held by the men of the upper middle class would make a more just society, it would only do so, obviously, for the members of the upper middle class. It would do no good at all for the people most conspicuously absent in elite science departments, the people who come from the bottom (or even the bottom half) of American society.

When we recast the issue of faculty diversity from the standpoint of the problem of economic inequality, we can see immediately both why the issue is such a popular one at universities and why it is utterly empty as a way of distinguishing between the right and the left. Or, rather, why it marks the degree to which the supposed left has turned into something like the human resources department of the right, concerned to make sure that the women of the upper middle class have the same privileges as the men. The reason is that it involves no redistribution of wealth whatsoever. And when feminist issues do get raised with respect to money, they tend to be equally irrelevant to the goal of economic equality. In a much-noted sexual discrimination case in 2004, for example, the banking firm Morgan Stanley settled before going to court with the lead plaintiff, its former employee Allison Schieffelin. Schieffelin had worked at Morgan Stanley for fourteen years but had been fired, she alleged, after complaining to the Equal Opportunity Employment Commission about discriminatory behavior that had led to her making less money than the men she worked with. For example, they were able to take the male clients on certain kinds of "men's only" "outings" while telling her, "explicitly or implicitly," to "go home."[3] When Schieffelin got $12 million, and a number of other women received substantial settlements as part of the agreement, and the brokerage house also agreed to spend $2 million on new "diversity programs," it certainly was a victory for diversity. But it was no victory for equality—unless you think the fact that Schieffelin was only making a little over $1 million per year selling bonds before she filed her suit and will now be a lot better off, while the company that discriminated against her will be a little worse off (its projected quarterly profit of something like $1 billion will be a bit down),[4] counts as a blow for equality.

"Diversity is always enhanceable," remarked the lead lawyer for Morgan Stanley, declining to admit that her client had been indifferent to diversity but suggesting that it was eager to do even better. And why shouldn't it be? The commitment to diversity doesn't threaten its profits; the feminism that demands that the women who sell bonds be treated as well as the men who sell bonds doesn't either. So there's no bad faith when the chairman of Morgan Stanley can announce that the company is "proud of our commitment to diversity" and when Schieffelin can praise the settlement as a "great" one "that's good for everybody."[5] The $2 million going to the new diversity programs will be money well spent, making sure that men who make $1.5 million a year learn how to treat women who make $1.3 million a year in a manner that guarantees them too the opportunity to earn $1.5 million. It's like a workplace version of the dancing class I went to as a kid: what they taught us then was not to let any girl be a wallflower; now, if you're working for Morgan Stanley, you learn not to dump her in a cab while you and your "male coworkers" take "the client to a strip club." The point here is not that it's OK for bond salesmen to make more than bond saleswomen or to behave badly to bond saleswomen (any more than it was OK for the boys in dancing class to behave badly). The point instead is that nothing about this victory for diversity, this "watershed in safeguarding and promoting the rights of women," has any connection to the liberal goal of creating a more economically equal society. Or, to put it another way, insofar as winning this bias suit counts as a victory for liberalism, it's only because liberalism has itself given up the goal of creating a more economically equal society. Redistributing wealth is one thing; making sure that the women of the upper class are paid just as well as the men of the upper class is another.

The idea here is not, of course, that feminism is intrinsically bad, any more than my critique of antiracism was meant to count as a defense of racism. The idea is rather that our efforts to solve the problem of discrimination—indeed, our formulation of the problem *as* a problem of discrimination—is not so much a contribution to justice as it is a way of accepting injustice. Compare the mistreated bond saleswomen with the women of Wal-Mart. The average hourly salary of a full-time Wal-Mart employee (according to the CEO of Wal-Mart) is about ten dollars.[6] So if you work a forty-hour week, you make $400 a week, almost $21,000 a year. The women who are victims of discrimination are making a little less, the men a little more; the difference between them, according to Richard Drogin, the statistician who ran the numbers for the discrimination suit, is (for hourly workers) $1,100 a year.[7] So let's say the Wal-Mart women are making about $20,500. It would take them sixty years to make what the Wall Street woman—also the victim of discrimination—makes in one year. Of course, the Wal-Mart men—the beneficiaries of that discrimination, they're making $21,600—do better; it would only take them about fifty-seven years to catch up with Wall Street. At Wal-Mart, in other words, you've got women struggling for a fair slice of a pie so small that it won't feed them even if they get it. It's ludicrous to think of them as standing shoulder to shoulder with their sisters at Morgan Stanley and at Harvard. It's ludicrous to think of their problem as a problem about gender. The men can't live on their salaries either! Laws against discrimination by gender are what you go for when you've given up on—or turned against—the idea of a strong labor movement. Feminism is what you appeal to when you want to make it sound as if the women of Wall Street and the women of Wal-Mart are both victims of sexism. Which is to say, when you want to disguise the fact that the women of Wall Street are not victims at all.

And just as rich people's problems can be given a certain respectability if they're redescribed as women's problems, gender can also be invoked as a way of concealing or misdescribing the reality of poor people's problems. The literature on domestic abuse, for example, regularly reminds us that this crime occurs at every level of American society, and there is a sense in which this is true, or at least about as true as the claim that there are rich people and poor people at Harvard. Rich women are sometimes abused, and poor children sometimes find their way into the Ivy League. But even though, as a paper by Amy Farmer and Jill Tiefenthaler puts it, "domestic violence claims victims in all races and socio-economic classes," the real point of their analysis is that "some women are more likely to be victims of abuse than others."[8] In particular, "women in the lowest income households have 7 times the abuse rates of those in the highest income household." So the insistence that women of every class are the victims of domestic abuse masks the fact that the great majority of victims are poor and that partner abuse is above all a crime of poverty. What's happening here is a kind of inversion of the rich-and-poor-at-Harvard effect, since the goal is not to make poor people more visible than they really are but to make them less visible, to mobilize middle- and upper-middle-class action against domestic violence by identifying it as a significant problem for the middle and upper middle classes.

Thus the idea that domestic violence is "confined" to lower-income families is regularly denounced as a "myth." Indeed, the "myth" "that victims of abuse come from lower-income families with little education" is the very first one listed by the columnist and religious leader Kerby Anderson in his inventory of mistaken beliefs about domestic violence. "In reality," Anderson says, "victims of domestic violence come from all walks of life."[9] But this, as we have seen, is only technically true. It's not a myth that the vast majority of domestic abuse victims *are* in lower-income families, and the effects of insisting that it is are often counterproductive. For example, one of the main findings of the study I cited above is that facilities to help the victims of domestic violence are disproportionately located in wealthier areas, that in fact there's an almost inverse relationship between the location of such facilities and the location of the population that needs them. But there is, of course, a deeper difficulty as well. By disconnecting the problem of domestic violence from the question of social class, we find ourselves misunderstanding and misrepresenting the problem itself. We fail to see that the problem of domestic violence is importantly a function of the problem of economic inequality; we fail to see that in a society with less poverty there would be less domestic violence. In other words, we take a problem that significantly involves people's economic status and pretend instead that it's a problem about the relations between the sexes. The social message of the campaign against domestic violence is thus that economic inequality is irrelevant; it becomes another way of convincing ourselves that the fundamental problems of American society have nothing to do with the injustices of capitalism and everything to do with the injustices (in this case) of sexism.

So domestic abuse is essentially a poor people's problem, like bad schooling and inadequate health care. Rich people's problems involve things like having to work very long hours and having to move every few years to keep climbing the corporate ladder. One of the featured couples in the *New York Times* series *Class Matters* "complains of stress and anomie," and the demands not just on the husband's time but also on the wife's.[10] Beyond volunteering at the children's school, taking them to soccer, fund-raising for cheerleading, and so forth, Mrs. Link attends a Bible study group ("two hours on Tuesday mornings") and plays in "three or four tennis leagues." At least politics doesn't take up too much time. In Alpharetta, Georgia, the suburb the *Times* selected to represent the hundreds of others just like it, "Republican candidates are shoo-ins. Few Alpharetta lawns sprouted campaign signs in November because the area's four contenders for the state legislature were all Republicans and ran unopposed."[11] The stress and anomie are at least partially compensated for by all the things salaries like Mr. Link's $200,000 a year can buy: the big houses (the Links' is five thousand square feet), the good schools, the country club, the soccer league, the piano lessons and special tutoring for the kids, the tennis for Mrs. Link, in general, the comfort. "The good thing about [Alpharetta] is that it is a very comfortable neighborhood to live in," Mr. Link says.

The bad thing, he says, is that "we're never challenged to learn much about other economic groups. . . . When you talk about tennis, guess what? Everybody you play against looks and acts and generally feels like you. You don't get much of a perspective." The problem here is economic segregation: the Links live with and socialize with people who belong to their own "economic group," and the lack of nearby housing affordable for poorer people means that they have no social relations with such people. Of course, they still have *some* relation to poorer people; it's the poorer people who clean their houses and take care of their gardens and work at their supermarkets. But the kids don't go to schools with poor people; the parents don't play tennis with poor people; there are no weekend barbecues with poor people. This truly is a rich people's problem; the rich people would like a broader experience of life, but they can't get it without having some poor people around.[12]

Indeed, although I argued in the previous chapter that the most powerful function of the commitment to diversity in universities was the legitimating one—convincing rich white people that they had arrived there on merit—the justification the schools actually give is the wider experience of life that Mr. Link wants and that diversity is supposed to provide. When college administrators talk about the advantages of a more diverse student body from the racial standpoint, they make the argument that the university should look more like the actual world. And the argument that racial balance ignores class then gets met by the call to supplement cultural diversity with economic diversity.

At least at the university, however, there's some advantage for the very few poor people involved, since going to the rich kids' schools may well help them become less poor. It's harder to see how playing doubles with rich suburbanites will perform any comparable function for the suburban poor. This is not to say that the cities, although they are much more diverse, are any better for the poor. As someone who lives in downtown Chicago rather than some gated community in a midwestern version of Alpharetta (say, Naperville), I may feel and actually be more in touch with the diversity of American life, but it's hard to see how my experience of diversity does much good for the homeless guy I walk past on my way to the El. More generally, the value of mixing rich people and poor people is real only if it contributes to the poor people becoming less poor, which is to say, if it *decreases* economic diversity. Indeed, since economic diversity is just another name for economic inequality, it's hard to see why we would want to promote it. We ought to want to get rid of it or at least to minimize it.

◆

Although Mr. Link worries about the lack of diversity in his neighborhood at home, he doesn't worry about it on the job, where, as he says, "diversity is one of the biggest things we work on." And not just, or even mainly, economic diversity. Mr. Link works for Wachovia Bank, an organization that describes its "commitment to diversity" as "a business imperative," that has a "Corporate Diversity Council" chaired not by some second-tier human resources person but by its CEO and that, on June 1, 2005, the very day the *Times* ran its story about Mr. and Mrs. Link, found itself publicly apologizing "to all Americans, and especially to African-Americans and people of African descent," for some of its past diversity shortcomings, in particular for the fact that two of its "predecessor institutions," the Georgia Railroad and Banking Company and the Bank of Charleston, "owned slaves."[13]

"The first thing I want to do," said the CEO (Ken Thompson) to his employees, "is apologize to each one of you and especially our African-American teammates." Such apologies have become increasingly popular in the last few years, and there is no reason to doubt that when companies declare themselves, as Wachovia did, "deeply saddened" by the discovery of slavery in their corporate heritage, they mean it. Indeed, apologizing for something you didn't do to people to whom you didn't do it (in fact, to people to whom it wasn't done) is something of a growth industry. A few months before Wachovia, JPMorgan apologized for having accepted slaves as collateral on mortgages (it "wound up owning about 1,250 of them when borrowers defaulted"). Morgan is "a very different company today" and "slavery was tragically ingrained in American society," said the letter sent to staff and shareholders, "but that is no excuse."[14] And Lehman Brothers had led the way a couple of years earlier, acknowledging past ties to slavery and then, in 2005, apologizing for the fact that in 1850 the founding brothers had bought a woman named Martha.

The Lehman Brothers experience, however, was in some ways a cautionary one. Their discoveries were so meager—essentially, Martha—that the response ("They had two years to do their research. . . . They're playing with us") was a little skeptical.[15] Wachovia and JPMorgan, by contrast, had the good sense to go straight to one of the "heritage management firms" that have come into existence over the last twenty-five years. JPMorgan worked with History Associates, which employs over fifty people (qualifications for entry-level employees include a B.A. in history). History Associates did some 3,500 hours of research for them. Wachovia hired the History Factory, which produced a 109-page report.[16] Founded by Bruce Weindruch (*Forbes* magazine calls him the man who's "Making History Pay"), the History Factory describes itself as a "heritage management firm" that can help you "turn to history" in order to enhance your "corporate culture" and your bottom line.[17] In the 1980s, when *In Search of Excellence* was the management bible, the company spent a lot of time combing through its clients' archives for examples of "excellent behavior."[18] Nowadays, since the city of Chicago passed its Slavery Era Disclosure Ordinance requiring all corporations doing business with Chicago to disclose any links they may have had to slavery or the slave trade, examples of unexcellent behavior are more apropos. The History Factory can still provide you with research for "heritage-based events" (retirements, mergers, anything involving your corporate identity) that go beyond having to say you're sorry, but if you want to get your share of lucrative codevelopment projects with the city of Chicago (it was Chicago alderman Dorothy Tillman who refused to accept

Lehman Brothers' apology), finding something you're sorry for is the way to go.

Of course, the ordinance just requires the disclosure, not the apology, but the corporations are only too happy to apologize. And, as I've already suggested, there's no reason to doubt their sincerity, or at least there's no reason to think that Ken Thompson and Wachovia are being hypocritical when they say they're sorry that the Bank of Charleston accepted slaves as collateral on loans. They're certainly not proud of it; after all, no one approves of slavery now. At the same time, however, it's hard to see why such an apology is worth having, a fact that's brought out by its scope—Wachovia apologizes to "all Americans"—as if white Americans were victims of slavery too. The real point is that, since none of the people apologizing for slavery actually owned slaves and since none of the people to whom they're apologizing (black or white) actually were slaves, the apology functions as a general statement of disapproval. And as long as progressive politics consists of disapproving of bad things that happened a long time ago, it isn't all that hard for corporations like Wachovia and JP-Morgan to be just as PC as the city councils (not only in Chicago but in Philadelphia, Los Angeles, and Berkeley, among others) with whom they're doing business.

But, of course, the Berkeley and Chicago laws that require disclosure also embody a financial hope. They have been generated as part of the reparations movement, and the hope is that they will lead to a victory for diversity more along the lines of Allison Schieffelin's, one that has some money attached to it. When History Associates found evidence of JPMorgan's involvement in the slave trade, Morgan produced $5 million for minority scholarships. Due to the hard work of six-figure-salary men like Mr. Link, Wachovia's after-tax profits in 2004 were more than $5 billion; it wouldn't be unreasonable to hope that this company too might come up with a little something. More ambitious hopes for corporate retributions, however—at least in the United States and for slavery—have failed, defeated above all by the argument, already suggested above, that the presumed plaintiffs (African Americans today) have no standing (since they weren't the ones enslaved) and that the targets of the suits (today's corporate officers and shareholders) cannot be held financially responsible (since they weren't the ones doing the enslaving). But, as a moment's thought will suggest, the argument for holding corporations like Wachovia (or, for that matter, the U.S. government) financially responsible doesn't really depend on their current officers and shareholders either being or feeling guilty. In fact, the argument for making them pay is much stronger than the argument for making them apologize.

Suppose your parents owned a valuable painting and/or deposited money in a secret savings account. Suppose the painting was stolen and your parents murdered by the thief; suppose the money in the secret account was kept by the bank. Suppose further that no one tried to do anything about this for, say, half a century, so not only have your parents (the victims) been dead for a long time, so has their murderer. The bank has been using the money; the painting's been sold and is now hanging in an art museum. Just like the slaveholders, the people who did the bad things can't be punished. But their descendants can give back the money they should never have had. Apologies are irrelevant, but restitution is not. Apologies are irrelevant because people can't feel too sorry about things they didn't do; restitution is relevant because they can give back money they should never have had. This is a distinction—between being guilty of committing the crime and being responsible for returning the property—that conservatives like Thomas Sowell, complaining about the "assumption of collective guilt,"[19] completely miss. But the museums that, finding themselves in possession of paintings stolen by the Nazis from Holocaust victims, have begun returning them to the victims' heirs, understand it. As do the Swiss banks that once refused to identify, much less release, the deposits of Holocaust victims but are now making a settlement of $1.25 billion (about a fifth of Wachovia's after-tax profit in 2004), "the bulk of which," as one of the victims' lawyers, Burt Neuborne, claims, "will go to the heirs of the original depositors."[20] If you support reparations not just to the victims of the Nazis but also to their heirs, there are no coherent grounds for opposing reparations to the heirs of slavery's victims.

Hence the most important polemicist for reparations, Randall Robinson, makes a good point when he argues (in his book *The Debt*) that "as Germany and other interests that profited *owed* reparations to Jews . . . America and other interests that profited *owe* reparations to blacks."[21] Of course, what was stolen from the slaves and from those who lived under Jim Crow is less concrete than bank accounts or works of art; it was more like first the right and then the opportunity to acquire those things. Slaves couldn't own property; the victims of Jim

Crow were denied the opportunity to acquire it. But although rights and opportunities are not quite as tangible as paintings, it's hard to deny that what Robinson correctly describes as "the socioeconomic gap between the races" in the United States today "derives from the social depredations of slavery." Even if we agree that African Americans today are not themselves the victims of slavery and racism, we can't plausibly deny that the economic circumstances of African Americans today are importantly a consequence of slavery and past racism. We can't plausibly deny, that is, that the economic disadvantages under which slaves labored were passed on to their children and that the new economic disadvantages (those produced as well as maintained by Jim Crow) under which the slaves' children labored have been passed on to their children. Indeed, even if we think—with right-wing polemicists like Dinesh D'Souza— that the problems of African Americans today derive not from racism but from the "pathology" of their culture, where are we to believe the culture came from? Robinson imagines for us the case of a little girl—he calls her Sarah—falling farther and farther behind in school because (as he sees it) her mother is too poor and too overworked to provide her with the support the other kids get or because (as the school sees it) her mother doesn't care enough about the child's progress in school, misses appointments with the teachers and doesn't read to her at home. Robinson blames the society; the school (like D'Souza) blames the mother. But we don't have to choose between them to realize that, whoever's fault it is, it's not Sarah's.

Whether we blame Sarah's failure on her poverty or on the "pathology" of her culture, we can't possibly blame it on her.

She didn't make herself poor; she didn't create her culture. Her situation is the effect of a cause, the product of a history that ended before she was ever born. It is this history—the history of slavery, Jim Crow and their aftermath—that produced what Robinson accurately characterizes as the "yawning economic gap between whites and blacks in this country," and the purpose of reparations is to undo the consequences of these events. Hence one of the standard objections to reparations—we didn't hold slaves; we're not racists—is completely irrelevant. The whole idea of reparations assumes that Sarah's problem is not continuing racial discrimination (if it were, the proper response would be just to stop the discrimination) but is instead the effect of past discrimination. The point is rather to undo as far as possible the consequences of the past; reparations are a technology for trying to create a world that comes as close as possible to the world we would have had if neither slavery nor Jim Crow had happened.

What if we actually got such a technology? Imagine a Martian comes down to Earth and we show him our problem. African Americans today constitute about 13 percent of the American population. But they currently make up a disproportionately large segment (around 32 percent) of the poorest quintile of the population. And they make up a disproportionately small segment (1.7 percent) of the households in the top 5 percent. The Martian uses his powers, and we make the economic effects of slavery and Jim Crow, the disproportion in American wealth, disappear. Now, just as 13 percent of America's population is black, 13 percent of America's poor people are black, and 13 percent of America's rich people are black.

We wave good-bye to the Martian and thank him . . . but for what? It's not as though America has been magically transformed into a more economically equal society; post-reparations America is exactly as unequal as prereparations America. Our Martian changed the skin color of many of America's poor and some of its rich, but he didn't change the division of wealth. So all we're thanking him for is eliminating racial inequality in the division of wealth. The economic gap between rich and poor remains, but the economic gap between black and white is gone.[22]

Is this a good thing? Well, the obvious objection is that leaving the economic inequalities of American society intact while rearranging the skin color of those who suffer from and those who benefit from those inequalities doesn't exactly count as progress. And certainly not if what we are seeking is economic equality. But the problem the movement sets out to solve has nothing to do with economic inequality. Reparations are compensatory; they give you back what you lost. Robinson's primary concern, then, is neither with equality nor even with the mere fact of poverty but with the poverty produced by slavery. He supports reparations because reparations would return to the descendants of the slaves at least some of what is rightfully theirs. The injustice he sets out to correct is that people had their property taken from them; the justice he hopes to provide is giving it back to them. "Lamentably," Robinson says, "there will always be poverty." But because the poverty that survives will not be the consequence of some past injustice, it will not in itself be unjust.

This is a familiar position, if not necessarily a familiar

position of the left. In fact, insofar as it relies on the idea that in a just society we owe Sarah the property to which she has a right, the property that would be hers if it hadn't been stolen from her ancestors, it's a conservative position, one with no connection to the goals of alleviating either poverty or inequality. When we're returning stolen property, we don't care whether the stolen painting belonged to a rich person or a poor person; your claim to the painting is based neither on your poverty nor on your wealth. No one today is more committed to property rights than the reparations movement, and conservatives who share that commitment ought to be its most outspoken defenders. They could even appeal to remarks by the most influential conservative philosopher of the last half century, Robert Nozick, who suggested that the "descendants" of "victims" of "the most serious injustice" would be "owed compensation" by "those who benefited from the injustice."[23]

The principle here is that injustices ought to be rectified, and the fact that they happened in the past does not alter that principle. It's a conservative principle because it relies on the appeal to the restoration of stolen property, whether it's the labor of slaves or the possessions of murdered Jews. And its application need not be so narrow. It isn't just African Americans and Jews who are the descendants of injustice. What about Native Americans? What about Appalachian coal miners and poor white sharecroppers? Once you start looking for past injustice, you don't have a hard time finding it. And, by the same token, you may well find it where you don't really feel you need it. Critics of reparations for slavery sometimes complain that the rich descendants of former slaves would benefit from reparations as much as the poor ones would. But rich people are just as entitled to the restoration of their property as poor people are; anyone prepared to give the equivalent of forty acres and a mule to the homeless man across the street ought to be just as happy to give it to Tiger Woods.

Nevertheless, because the Tiger Woodses of this world are statistically a very small group, it makes sense for those of us who are interested in a more equal distribution of wealth to support reparations. A lot more of the money would go to poor people than to rich people. But it's more important to recognize that there is nothing egalitarian about the principle of reparations and to see that the injustice done to little girls like Sarah has nothing to do with them being descended from the victims of past injustice. Indeed, it has nothing to do with the past at all.

Suppose, for example, that I am Sarah's white friend. My father wasn't a slave but was instead a slaveholder. Suppose that, when slavery was abolished, the Radical Republican plans to divide the plantations among the slaves who had worked on them had been put into effect and my slaveholding father lost not only all his slaves but all his land too. Suppose, left destitute, he turned to drink and abandoned my pregnant mother, who was left to raise me without the ability either to support me (since she'd never worked a day in her life) or to care for me (since slaves had done the child rearing in her family). Suppose now, at nine years old, I'm not doing so well in school. My work habits are bad; my mother's too depressed to read with me; my reading proficiency scores are plummeting. Do I deserve reparations? Obviously not. What would they be reparations for? My ancestors weren't kidnapped and enslaved; just the opposite—they were the ones who did the kidnapping and enslaving. The advocates of reparations describe what they would call Sarah's history (i.e., the history of her ancestors) as a mixture of suffering and nobility; my equivalent is a mixture of exploitation and rapacity. So with respect to the historical claims of the reparations movement, I'm completely different from Sarah. But I am no more responsible for my poverty than Sarah is. I don't deserve compensation, but does that mean I deserve my poverty?

There are two ways in which we can understand our responsibility to children like Sarah. One is to say that in a just society we owe her the property she ought to have had. The other is to say that in a just society we owe her an opportunity as equal as we can make it to the opportunities of all the other children. And if equality of opportunity is our idea of justice, the history of how you came to be born poor may be of interest to you and your loved ones and the other members of your family, but it has nothing to do with the relevant fact about you: the fact that you are not yourself responsible for your poverty. And our responsibility to you has nothing to do with that history either. Indeed, the idea of equal opportunity, if it were taken seriously, would make all the histories of victimization and the subsequent demands for compensation irrelevant, just as—again, if it were taken seriously—it would make the histories of accumulation irrelevant. Rich children are no more responsible for their advantages than poor ones are for their disadvantages. We've already had occasion to question the current obsession with history, and here's another one: it's powerfully tied to the idea of people getting what they deserve when what they deserve is identified with inherited property rather than with equal opportunity.

But if we do take seriously not just the commitment to private property that reparations relies on but also our commitment to equality of opportunity, a commitment that virtually every American is eager to endorse, things change. The whole point of the commitment to equal opportunity is to make sure not only that people have a right to their property but also that they have a fair chance to earn that property. Only if everybody has a chance to get rich can the people who don't get rich, the people who stay poor, be said to deserve their poverty. And only if everybody has a chance to get rich can the people who do succeed be said to deserve their wealth.

It's often said—both in defense and in criticism—that equality of opportunity is the weakest form of egalitarianism. The strongest form would be equality of outcome. And it's obviously true that a world in which everyone was required to finish the race at the same time would be very different from a world in which everyone was required to start it at the same time. To justify equality of outcome, we have to think that there should be no reward for hard work or ability. Whereas in fact what most of us think is that there should be some such reward. Indeed, we defend equality of opportunity precisely because we believe that if people don't begin with equal opportunities to succeed, hard work and ability won't be rewarded. If, for example, my wealth enables my daughter to be tracked from birth into an elite college while your daughter is tracked from birth into a community college or no college at all, my wealth (and my education and all the other things that we generally use to measure socioeconomic status) is doing at least part of the job that my daughter's hard work and ability ought to be doing. So our commitment to equal opportunity requires us to refuse equality of economic outcome (because that doesn't reward hard work and ability), and it also requires us to refuse the generational transfer of economic inequality—for the very same reason (it doesn't reward hard work and ability).

When the point is put that way, we can also see that the commitment to equality of opportunity is not really a weaker form of the commitment to equality of outcome; rather, it's a commitment to something altogether different, to the importance of hard work and ability. And we can also see that, genuinely implemented, it's not so weak. For example, a society that really was as committed to equal opportunity as we say we are would not allow the quality of local schools to be dependent on local real estate taxes. If the schools are better where the rich people live, the unearned advantage their children have starts at pre-K. And, of course, it's precisely to provide that unearned advantage that people like the constantly relocating Links make the quality of the schools the "number one" criterion whenever they move. There's nothing surprising or irrational or immoral about this. Almost any parent, given unequal schools and given the ability (i.e., the money) to choose between them, will choose the good one for his or her children. In fact the immorality, if there is any, seems to be on the other side. How, if you have the opportunity to send your children to the good school, can you justify sending them to the bad one? This is the kind of dilemma that public figures, especially in major cities, frequently confront.

But to think of this as an ethical decision for individual parents is to miss the point of the problem, which, if all school districts were funded equally (and if there were no private schools), would begin to look very different. If no school were better or worse than any other, it wouldn't matter which one your children went to. So if we really are committed to equality of opportunity, the relevant choice we make as parents is not between schools but between ways of funding them. If we are committed to equality of opportunity, we should be funding all school districts equally and abolishing private schools, thus removing the temptation for rich parents to buy their children an unfair advantage. But we don't do this, and we can't even imagine it on a ballot.

There are, of course, even more blatant violations of the commitment to equal opportunity. The majority of Americans, for instance, think there should be no inheritance tax, that is, they think that hard work and ability should make no difference whatsoever when it comes to distributing the billions of dollars that change hands from one generation to another. And another 20 percent think that only estates above $3.5 million should be taxed.[24]

How do we explain this? How do we explain the simultaneous commitment to the importance of hard work and ability (making your money) and to the irrelevance of hard work and ability (inheriting it)? People who are opposed to the inheritance tax are not being hypocritical, choosing their pocketbooks over their principles. Almost none of the 50 percent of the population that opposes the inheritance tax no matter how big the estate is will ever see a dime's worth of taxable inheritance. On the contrary, the vast majority of people who oppose inheritance taxes are taking positions of pure principle, advocating that people with advantages they themselves never had (like going to the best schools and to elite universities) not only reap the rewards of those advantages but reap them again when their parents die. These people are acting against their own economic interests and on behalf of what seems to them fair: the principle that people should be allowed to do what they like with their money, including passing it on untaxed to their children. But that notion of fairness completely contradicts the principle of equal opportunity.

When it comes to choosing between a world in which people can do whatever they want with their money and a world of equal opportunity, when it comes to choosing between a world in which hard work and ability matter less than inheritance and a world in which they matter more, we seem to be choosing inheritance. So maybe we have to conclude that we Americans just aren't all that committed to equal opportunity after all. But this is a conclusion that's hard to accept. For what is there to justify our respect for other people's property (and our laws protecting that property) if we don't believe that hard work and ability played a central role in earning it? "Equality of opportunity is a demanding standard," as two writers for a conservative think-tank, the American Enterprise Institute, recently observed, and an important one, since "people must believe that our system is generally fair for it to remain vital."

"If this belief no longer exists," they conclude, if people no longer "perceive the rules of the game to be fair, . . . the political repercussions could be significant."[25]

This is a polite way of putting a point that could be made more bluntly. If you have a political system that is constructed to benefit a certain group of people regardless of their natural ability (we don't mind the most talented players winning the game) and regardless of their energy and commitment (we don't mind the hardest workers earning the rewards), why shouldn't you just tear it down? The book in which the point is made is called *Attitudes Toward Economic Inequality*, and it's a survey of polls conducted over the last half century, measuring Americans' feelings about the fact that some people have more money and more property than others. The data, from the standpoint of the authors, are mostly reassuring. Respondents overwhelmingly (between 75 percent and 80 percent) agree with statements like "People who work hard in this nation are likely to succeed" and only somewhat less enthusiastically give positive answers to questions like "How good a chance do you think a person has to become rich today, if the person is willing to work hard?" In 1990, over half the country thought a hard worker had a "very good" or "good" chance to become rich. These questions are, in effect, measuring two things: first, people's sense that what the authors call the rules of the game are fair and, second, their sense that, because the rules are fair, most people have a good chance to succeed. The more recent *New York Times*/CBS poll largely supports these findings. Where 44 percent of the respondents think that coming from a wealthy family is either "essential" or "very important" to "getting ahead," 87 percent think "hard work" is essential or very important (and 85 percent think a good education is).

What makes these polls reassuring from the conservative standpoint is not just the evidence they provide that we Americans still believe in the ideal of equality of opportunity but also the evidence they provide that we also believe it is a reality. We believe, in other words, that rich people today mainly deserve their wealth. This explains the lack of what the American Enterprise authors call class "resentment." More generally, it helps clarify (what many writers have recently found puzzling) why so many poor people continuously vote against their own economic interests. The most popular explanation here has been the so-called culture wars; the idea is that poor and lower-middle-class people have been convinced by conservatives that "culture outweighs economics as a matter of public concern," and that, as a result, they have increasingly voted for people they agree with on such issues as abortion, homosexuality, and prayer in schools and have thus voted against their own economic interests. As Thomas Frank sums it up in *What's the Matter with Kansas?* what we have is a "contradiction"—"a working-class movement that has done incalculable harm to working-class people."[26]

But, of course, the phenomenon of people voting against their economic interests is a pretty familiar one. Every time I have voted for someone who advocated higher taxes on the upper middle class (or at least was opposed to lowering them—it's become increasingly hard to find even Democrats who are committed to raising them), I have voted against my economic interests. And there isn't really any contradiction in thinking that it's more important to stop abortion than it is to further your economic interests. There's not even any contradiction in thinking that it's more important to eliminate the estate tax (an act that benefits only the rich) when you are yourself poor, would never have had to pay such a tax anyway, and might have benefited from the money the tax would raise. If you think the tax is wrong, you're right to be against it—whether or not it's in your interest. The real contradiction is between our support for equal opportunity and our support for all the things that make our opportunities unequal. So it won't work just to convince people that they're acting against their own economic interests. The point must be to convince them that they're acting unjustly.

5

Who Are We? Why Should We Care?

In January 2006, Evo Morales was inaugurated as the new president of Bolivia, twice. Once was in La Paz, the capital, where, wearing a dark suit (but no tie, as befits his populist image), he was sworn in before thousands of Bolivians and the representatives of many other governments. The other time—it was actually the day before—was about forty miles from La Paz, in Tiwanaku, among the ruins of Bolivia's major pre-Columbian city. This time he was barefoot and dressed in the red robes worn by pre-Incan sun priests. In La Paz, he took the oath of office in Spanish; in the ruins of the temple at Tiwanaku, he was, according to the *Daily Telegraph*, "invested with sacred powers by two shamans using the indigenous Aymara language."[1] On both occasions, however, he vowed to resist globalization and neoliberalism.

How successful Morales will be in opposing globalization,

I have no idea. My interest here is in the two different constit-
uencies represented by the two inaugurations, and in the two
very different ideas of resistance implied by them. The party
Morales leads is the MAS party. (MAS is the acronym for Mov-
imiento al Socialismo, movement toward socialism.) He is
also the first indigenous head of the Bolivian state in over four
hundred years, since the Spanish conquest. Practically speaking, there's clearly a significant overlap between these two
things in Bolivia today (Morales got 54 percent of the vote). But
there's also a significant difference. To be a socialist is to have
an ideology. Socialists believe in some of the things Morales
believes in, like nationalizing the Bolivian water system, which
had, at the urging of the International Monetary Fund, been
privatized. To be an Aymara Indian is to have not an ideology
but an identity. When Morales talks about "nationalizing industry," he is speaking as a socialist; when he talks about fulfilling the dreams "of our ancestors," he is speaking as an
Indian. The ancestors of many members of MAS (the non-
indigenous "middle class, the working class, the profession-
als, even the businessmen" whom he thanked in his inaugural
speech) no doubt had exactly the opposite dreams.

This difference—between who your ancestors are and what
your beliefs are—functions in much the same way as the difference between who your ancestors are and how much money
you have. Both work to obscure the fundamental problem of
economic inequality. A socialist and an Indian can fight for the
same cause but for different reasons. Here, for example, are
two reasons you might want to resist the privatization of water
rights. You might, if you're a socialist, want to minimize cor-

porate ownership of public utilities. You might, if you're an Indian, want to hang on to what an article in the journal *Cultural Survival* calls your "cultural traditions," distributing water in the way your ancestors did.[2] And although in this case, the different reasons lead to the same result, it's obvious that they needn't and often won't. If what you want is to preserve your identity, things like continuing to speak your native language will be crucial to you; the resistance of indigenous peoples to globalization is understood from this standpoint as their struggle "for the recognition of their cultural identity."[3] But if what you want is to promote socialism, you won't much care what language gets spoken; what you'll want is to find a "new economic model" to replace the neoliberal insistence on the primacy of the "private sector."

It's hard at this point to know which of these goals matters most to MAS, but the failure of neoliberal reforms in Argentina and the rise of a new leftism in Venezuela as well as in Bolivia suggest that politicians like Morales may be more interested in opposing capitalism than in fulfilling the dreams of their ancestors. They are not, of course, always required to choose between these goals. Bolivian socialists can continue to speak Aymara, and it may well be that if they want to win elections, they ought to, although, as we will see, there's nothing about hanging onto old identities that in itself counts as resistance to globalization.

In the United States, however, where the justice of the free market seems so incontrovertible that it renders new economic models almost literally unimaginable, the mainstream commitment to culture has produced an equally mainstream focus on the ancestors. The "emergence of a global economy," says the distinguished and influential political scientist Samuel P. Huntington, has created a "global identity crisis."[4] And, far from being at odds with neoliberalism, this diagnosis— whether we end up worrying about our own identity or the identity of others—is deeply compatible with it.

Indeed, not only do many prefer to think of the problem of globalization in terms of the threat it poses to diversity, they also prefer to understand our own political differences as differences in identity rather than ideology, as differences in who we are rather than in what we believe. This is strikingly visible on the extremes of American politics. The far right, for example, used to be identifiable by its obsessive anticommunism, a position that was obviously bound to lose some of its urgency and attractiveness after the fall of the Soviet Union. But even before the evil empire disappeared, the focus on political ideology had started to become an interest in racial identity. The literature of the old John Birch Society (founded by Robert Welch in 1958) concerned itself with the communist conspiracy run by "the vicious savages of the Kremlin"; by the late 1970s, the literature of the radical right focused not on communists but on blacks and Jews. In fact, William L. Pierce, the author of *The Turner Diaries*, tells of having gone to a Birch Society meeting in the late 1960s and of being rebuffed when he started talking about race. According to the Birch Society, he complained, "Anyone who raised the race issue or the Jewish issue was probably a Communist agent trying to divide anti-Communist Americans along racial or ethnic lines."[5] Pierce wrote a letter to Welch, elaborating on his views, but Welch was unimpressed and at that point, says the future leader of what the Anti-Defamation League once called "the most dangerous organized hate group in the United States,"[6] "the John Birch Society and I parted company." The Birch Society's idea of a happy ending was the exposure and elimination of the "Communist conspiracy." Pierce's happy ending takes the Cold War scenario of a nuclear war against the communists and updates it as a "demographic war" against the nonwhite. The bad news is that "millions of racial kinsmen in the Soviet Union" (i.e., white guys now, not vicious savages) are unavoidably killed; the good news is that the ones who survive get right to work rounding up their remaining Jews and hurling them "into burning buildings or onto burning heaps of debris."[7]

The old right-wing extremists were committed to defending free enterprise; the new ones are committed to defending the white race. They aren't "soft-bellied, conservative businessmen"; they're "*real men, White men.*" You can't get a much better example of what it means to care about identity instead of ideology than the switch from conservative to white. But you can get some that are just as good. In Leslie Marmon Silko's novel *Almanac of the Dead*, a Cuban communist gets himself executed by the novel's Native American heroes because of his indifference to their history. He keeps telling them they're exploited and they should be fighting capitalism; they keep telling him they're not respected, and they want to fight white people. So when the Marxist carries on once too often about the evils of private property and won't stop to listen to stories about their heritage (the massacres, the thefts, the forced assimilation), they hang him for "crimes against [their] history."[8] What defines the Marxist is what he believes, but what defines the Indians is who they are. And Karl Marx himself, they think, was more like them—more a "tribal Jew" than a Marxist. He would have understood that the battle was not between socialism and capitalism but between indigenous people and Europeans. So just as Marxism doesn't matter to the racist right (it was nothing, according to Pierce, but "a Jewish power grab"), it doesn't matter to Silko and the multicultural left. The relevant thing in both cases is the Jewishness; the difference is that the racist right hates Jews while the multicultural left likes them.

But, of course, these are the extremes. Mainstream political thought in America is not the slightest bit anti-Semitic, and you will definitely not find anybody on the Sunday morning talk shows calling for a few "real men, White men" to get out on the streets and start lynching race-mixers. What you will find them worrying about, however, is what Huntington calls the "clash of civilizations," and if you read what he has written on the topic you will see that the basic idea—the idea that difference in identity now matters more than difference in belief—is pretty much the same in the center as it is on the margins. Huntington's point is that the fall of the Soviet Union produced a world in which the ideological conflict between socialism and liberal capitalism (the Cold War) has been replaced by conflict between civilizations. The "fundamental source of conflict in this new world will not be primarily ideological," he argues, but will instead be "cultural." In ideological conflicts, "the key question was 'Which side are you on?' and people could and did choose sides and change sides." You can, for example, be born into a communist society and become convinced of the virtues of capitalism. But cultural conflict, he thinks, is very different. "In conflicts between civilizations," as Huntington puts it, "the question is 'What are you?' not which side are you on," and what you are, he says, "is a given that can't be changed."[9] And even if it does somehow get altered, what's being changed is not your mind but something more fundamental, your self.

Think, for example, of the difference between being convinced (by someone else's argument) and being assimilated (into someone else's culture). None of the pathos that attaches to the loss of a culture attaches to the change in beliefs that's involved in losing an argument. How could it? Since the phenomenon of changing one's beliefs irreducibly involves the sense that the new beliefs are better than the old ones—after all, the new beliefs are ones that now seem to you right and the old ones seem wrong; that's why you changed them—it makes no logical and not much emotional sense to mourn the passing of the old beliefs. No one sits around wishing that we still thought human sacrifice was an effective way of propitiating the gods or that bad air caused malaria. But culture and cultural identity seem to us very different. Because we don't think of cultures as right or wrong, we don't necessarily experience the passage from one to another as progress. Another way to put this would be to say that people who hold different beliefs disagree; people who belong to different cultures differ without disagreeing. Indeed, just as the very idea of culture takes us away from the question of ideology (what we believe), so does the idea of cultural diversity. The alternative to diversity is sameness. So where beliefs are relevantly divided not into yours or mine but into right or wrong, the relevant axis of evaluation for cultures is not right or wrong but same or different. We can be plausibly urged to appreciate and even celebrate difference, but no one thinks we should appreciate mistakenness. Differences in belief, like differences in wealth, are not differences we can love.

But we can love the differences between cultures because cultures (and the identities they give us) make no claim to being either better or worse. They're just ours or not ours. Arthur Schlesinger Jr., like Huntington, has been an opponent of multiculturalism, but he exemplifies its basic tenets when, defending national identity against "ethnic and racial pride," he says that "we don't have to believe that our values are absolutely better than the next fellow's or the next country's, but we have no doubt that they are better *for us* . . . and that they are worth living and dying for."[10] Here multiculturalism and its opponents converge. The identity Schlesinger and Huntington want us to love is national; the ones multiculturalists want us to love are racial and ethnic. The basic idea, however, is the same: we love our own not because it's better but because it's "better for us," because it's ours. Thus Huntington's book *Who Are We?* is an argument for preserving those "qualities" that make America "different." "America cannot become the world and still be America," he writes. "Other peoples cannot become American and still be themselves."[11] What Huntington wants for Americans is what the titles of journals like *Cultural Survival* suggest the Aymara Indians want for themselves: to preserve their (and our) identities.

So what is it we want to preserve when we want to preserve our identities? Racists like Pierce have an easy answer to this question: they want to defend the purity of their "genetic heritage" against "mongrelization." But most of the people defending identity today are not racists. The answer to Huntington's question—"who are we?"—is not "white guys." And it's not capitalists either. The "Hispanization of Miami," which Huntington deplores, was produced by people whose anticommunist credentials are impeccable, but that doesn't make them any less a threat to American cultural identity; it's their Latin Americanness that's the problem. And the people who are most opposed to Huntington's idea of American identity aren't much interested in capitalism or communism either. In America, if not Bolivia, the real-life versions of Silko's Indians are as hostile to socialism as the fictional ones are. Ward Churchill, the Cherokee Indian best known now for his intemperate remarks about the chickens coming home to roost on 9/11, calls for an alternative to "*both* Marxism and capitalism" that he terms *indigenism*,[12] thus affiliating himself with a concept that has, as one of its historians says, gained an "ever-widening circulation" since the 1980s. The answer to the question "Who are we?" is increasingly, as Ronald Niezen says in *The Origins of Indigenism*, the naming of "an indigenous entity," the assertion "with pride" of a cultural identity.[13]

Hence the *Draft United Nations Declaration on the Rights of Indigenous Peoples* asserts that "indigenous peoples have the . . . right to maintain and develop their distinct identities and characteristics."[14] Needless to say, the identities that people like Churchill have in mind are Lakota and Inuit and Navajo-Hopi, and the UN isn't too worried about preserving the distinctive characteristics of Americans. But Huntington is. When he dedicates his *Who Are We?* "To Candace, Max, Eliza And Their American Futures," he's expressing exactly the same hope that's expressed by the idea of indigenism: the hope that the "distinctive" qualities of individual societies will survive, the hope not just (or not even) that Candace, Max and Eliza will continue to be happy and prosperous but that they will continue to be American. And when he goes on to express his concern above all about the "threat to English," he is speaking in terms that indigenists would find instantly recognizable. Huntington is interested also in religion, but language, he thinks, is "the basis of community," "the blood of the spirit."[15] If Americans stop speaking English, Huntington says, America will no longer be America. A "way of life disappears with the death of a language" is the way the authors of *Vanishing Voices: The Extinction of a World's Languages* put it.[16] The difference between Huntington and them is just that he fears the disappearance of English, and they fear the disappearance of everything else.

It's for this reason that Mark Abley, worried about the danger that globalization poses to "linguistic diversity" and "local cultures," begins his book of "travels among threatened languages" with the figure of an "old man" watching "a milky ocean roll in to the shore."[17] What's supposed to make the old man a tragic figure is not that he hasn't got any descendants (in fact, he's surrounded by his children and his grandchildren) but that he can't speak to them—or, anyway, he can't speak to them in his native language. The old man and his sister are the last speakers of an Australian aboriginal language called Mati

Ke. When they die, Mati Ke culture will die too.[18] So the (very plausible) worry is that, sooner or later, everybody in Australia will just speak English. And although Huntington's worry about the threat to English and to what he calls the "core culture" of America is less plausible—Spanish still has a ways to go—it's structurally the same. What if one day some "lone elder," maybe a professor emeritus at Harvard, should stand on the Massachusetts shore, watching not the Timor Sea but the Atlantic roll in? Wouldn't we feel bad if he were the last of the Americans, the last speaker of English, the last embodiment of American culture?

We can begin to understand what's at stake in this question if we go back for a moment to the last of the Mati Ke. Abley's lone elder is Patrick Nudjulu. He speaks at least four other languages (including English), and he sometimes tries to teach his grandchildren some Mati Ke, but it doesn't really take; they can understand a little of what he says, but they can't speak it back to him. So his native language is one that, Abley says, he can hear "only in his dreams." And this is true because, even though Agatha Perdjert, the other surviving speaker, doesn't live very far away and even though she's his sister, Patrick never talks to her. In fact, just because she's his sister, he's not *allowed* to talk to her. One part of Mati Ke culture is speaking Mati Ke; another part is "prohibiting a brother and sister from conversing after puberty." And when Patrick Nudjulu and his sister die, both parts will disappear. No one on this earth will speak Mati Ke anymore. And no brothers and sisters (or at least no Mati Ke brothers and sisters) will be prohibited from talking to each other after puberty.

It's not hard to see the difficulty here. The Mati Ke—
"indigenous people" in general—are frequently described as
people with traditional ways, concerned to keep their traditions
alive. And (unlike communists but just like Arthur Schlesinger
Jr.), the values they want to preserve are the values they think
of as "better for them." After all, that's what it means to want
to preserve your identity, to want to preserve the "distinctive"
character of your culture. People who are committed to an
ideology instead of an identity don't want to preserve difference; communists, for example, thought the abolition of private
property was right and they wanted everyone to give it up. But
the Mati Ke don't think that their language is either right or
wrong, and they don't care if anyone else speaks it; they just
want to be able to speak it themselves. Furthermore, they also
don't care if American brothers and sisters do or don't talk
to each other after puberty. They don't think it's wrong
for *all* brothers and sisters to talk to each other after puberty;
they just think it's wrong for them, for the members of Mati
Ke culture.

But here's where the problem comes in. We don't ordinarily accept the idea that identifying some practice as a part of
your culture counts in itself as a defense of your right to continue doing it, much less as support for the idea that you should
be able to make your children keep doing it. Of course, not
being allowed to talk to your sibling after puberty may not
seem really awful to us; it's just a little unfair. But what if we
tease it out a little? Because you can't talk to your brother, you
can't go to the school he goes to or you can't attend the public
meetings where he and the other men debate important issues.

Or what if we replace not talking to your sister with some of the social arrangements of different cultures, like not allowing the black people and the white people to sit next to each other on the bus or in the movie theater or in school? What if American segregationists had described themselves as participating in a culture of segregation and had said (which, sometimes, they did) that they didn't, of course, claim that segregation was good for everyone but they did claim it was good for them and that their culture had a right to survive? We wouldn't for a second accept that argument. We don't think that just redescribing people who believe in segregation as people whose culture is segregationist grants their beliefs a right to recognition and survival. Suppose someone says, "Look, I'm not claiming that segregation [or clitoridectomy or infanticide or, if you feel strongly about it, not talking to your brother] is absolutely better than other social practices; I'm just saying it's better for us, raised as we have been, with our traditions, et cetera." We don't think that statement counts as a defense of the practice in question. So even if we accept the idea that the big ideological differences don't matter anymore, and that what matters instead is identity, we don't accept the idea that all parts of a cultural identity are equally worthy of respect.

So what about speaking Mati Ke? It may not make sense to mourn the loss of the parts of Mati Ke culture that seem to us repressive and bad, but we can't possibly think of speaking Mati Ke as bad. Or at least we can't anymore. Not so long ago it was still widely believed that there were such things as "primitive" languages, languages that weren't as good as the more civilized ones. Abley gives the example of S. Hall Young, a missionary to the Tlingit Indians in Alaska who denounced the "barbarous practices" of the Tlingit, including the "barbarous sun dance, where he lacerates his flesh" and especially the "barbarous dialect" in which he talks to the other barbarians. "Barbarous," as Abley convincingly observes, "appears to have been his favorite word." But if there's one thing we've learned about languages in the last century, it's that there's no such thing as a barbarous one. "No language," as the linguist John Edwards has written, "can be described as better or worse than another on purely linguistic grounds," by which he means that all "languages are always sufficient for the needs of their speakers."[19] Patrick Nudjulu didn't stop speaking Mati Ke and start speaking English because English was better. And if he's sad because he now speaks more English than Mati Ke, it's not because English is worse.

This is why it does indeed make sense to respect linguistic difference. My language cannot be truer or better than yours; on what grounds, then (except maybe those of convenience), can I urge you to give up yours and start speaking mine? It's a mistake to think, as Schlesinger says, that our values can be best just for us, but it's not a mistake to think that our language can. So as long as we think of our culture along the lines of our language, it cannot be right for other people to try and take it away. The Reverend S. Hall Young was wrong to try to make the Tlingit stop speaking their language, and it would be wrong to try to force or even argue the Mati Ke out of speaking their language. On the other hand, and for the very same reason (the reason that no language is better or worse than any other language), it also doesn't make any sense for society to mourn the disappearance of Mati Ke. Patrick Nudjulu and his sister may be sad because they have no one to speak to in their native tongue, but their loss does not translate into any collective deprivation. For if cultures, like languages, are neither better nor worse than each other, whichever ones people end up with will be just as good as the ones their ancestors used to have.

And this goes for our own culture and our own language as well as for other people's. Suppose Huntington's worst fears come true, and it's English, not Mati Ke, that's under threat. As the Hispanic population of the United States keeps increasing, Spanish begins to be seen and heard everywhere; our children become bilingual; our grandchildren barely speak English, and our great-grandchildren don't speak it at all. English disappears, but so what? It's not as if democracy disappeared. That would be bad because our great-grandchildren would be living under a political system that was not just different from ours but worse. But Spanish isn't worse than English, and it's hard to see how the change in languages (as opposed to the change in ideologies) can count as a problem for anyone. We got to speak our language (English); our great-grandchildren get to speak their language (Spanish).[20]

The basic idea of the commitment to linguistic diversity is that linguistic diversity is a form of (really the primary form of) cultural diversity and that we should protect cultural diversity because to do so is to respect the cultural identity of others by treating them as we would wish to be treated ourselves. If "we're concerned with identity," as the philosopher Charles Taylor puts it, "then what is more legitimate than one's aspiration that it never be lost?"[21] Actually, however, the things that we don't want to lose are the things that have nothing to do with our identity. We don't, for example, want to lose great works of art—not because they're part of our culture but because they're great. If we just thought that Shakespeare was good *for us*, we would naturally want his plays around as long as we were around, but we wouldn't care if subsequent generations preferred, say, David Mamet. It's only because, rightly or wrongly, we think Shakespeare is good for everyone— regardless of identity—that we want his plays to survive. And we think works of art are different from languages precisely because, unlike languages, they *can* be better or worse.[22] If we really thought that every work of art (like every language) was just as good as every other work of art, it would indeed be hard to defend the idea that the works of art we happened to be familiar with should survive; there's no loss worth mourning if the things we love die with us and are just replaced by the things our descendants love instead.

And this is even more obviously true of other things we may value. If we live in liberal democracies and if we value the institutions that make those democracies possible, we can't help but wish for those institutions to survive. But we do so, of course, because we believe that those institutions are superior to others, which is to say, we believe, for example, that liberal capitalism is superior to socialism. Our desire, then (if it is our desire), is for liberal capitalism to survive because it seems to us good. It's a desire that can be understood only inasmuch as its object is not a culture, not an identity. This is why I argue that if the important thing about my culture is that it's mine, I can't really care if it survives. And this is also why we should get rid of the idea that the clash of cultures and the preservation of identities is what matters.

For one thing, the clash of cultures not only looks but is disingenuous; when we clash with others it's usually because we think we're right, not because we're defending our identity. When the International Monetary Fund tries to get Bolivia to privatize water rights, it's not an identity it's trying to impose, it's capitalism; the Bolivians are welcome to keep on speaking Aymara. And for another thing, insofar as culture really does work the way language does, identity politics are absolutely inconsequential. The advantage of culture over ideology is that we do not need to find reasons to defend our culture. The fact that it's ours is all that matters; the disadvantage is that once we describe the things we believe as expressions of our identity, we can't logically care whether anyone else does or will believe them. In Huntington's own terms: once we turn the clash of ideologies into the clash of civilizations, we can no longer care who will win; we have no reason to want any particular civilization, including our own, to survive. Theorists who defend cultural identity think of themselves as defending the right of cultures to survive. But if there really are such things as cultural identities, no one (not even the theorists who defend them) can possibly—or maybe I should say, coherently— care whether they survive.

I say *coherently* instead of *possibly* because it's obvious that people do feel quite strongly about the survival (and even the revival) of cultures even though, according to me, they shouldn't. Indeed, the end of the Cold War and what's now described as globalization (i.e., the penetration of capitalism into every part of the world) seem to be going hand in hand with an increasingly passionate commitment to culture. Greater indifference to inequality and ideology is happily accompanied by greater attachment to identity. In fact, this is what the commitment to diversity is all about, since a world of people who are different from us looks a lot more appealing than a world of people who are poorer than us or a world of people who think our fundamental beliefs are deeply mistaken. We might even say that this insistence on organizing the world around who we are rather than around what we have or what we believe is one of the defining features of globalization, of a post–Cold War world in which people who used to think of themselves as having an ideology—either capitalist or socialist—now think of themselves above all as having an identity: national, ethnic, cultural, whatever.

It isn't, of course, surprising that people who support globalization feel this way. We've already seen that the respect for difference is a powerful management tool, and, not surprisingly, it's even more important in marketing. If you try to sell snack foods as hors d'oeuvres in countries where they would more plausibly serve as "meal replacements," says the "Cultural Diversity in Snacking" Web site of Kerry Ingredients, your ignorance of "local culture" dooms you to failure. And even (or especially) Wal-Mart gets the point of cultural difference when it comes to sales: its "Wedding Day wishes, Mrs. & Mrs." and "Congratulations, Mr. & Mr." cards are available in England but not in Bentonville. Furthermore, consumers who want products appealing to their own cultures also want products representing other people's cultures. Starbucks everywhere will sell you Fair Trade coffee, made with beans grown by groups like the Mut Vitz cooperative in Mexico, whose members, their wholesaler proudly proclaims, "are living on their father's father's father's land" and are as committed to the "Zapatista movement for cultural survival and self-determination of indigenous peoples in Chiapas" as they are to providing you with a good cup of coffee.[23] And for tourism in places like Vietnam to continue its extraordinary growth (about 20 percent a year), the country's "charming" and "quite picturesque" "ethnic minorities" must flourish. So to "satisfy the need for entertainment and study of tourists," says Vu The Binh, the director of the Travel Department in Hanoi, Vietnam is "protecting the cultural identity and lifestyle of the ethnic groups."[24] The United States may have lost the war in Vietnam, but cultural identity, not communism, won.

It's pretty obvious, then, that when it comes to globalization, there's a big difference between dealing with indigenous peoples who want to protect their culture and socialists who want to nationalize your industry. Nevertheless, the protection of cultures often gets represented as if it were somehow a kind of *resistance* to globalization. Not, of course, an economic resistance. Ronald Niezen calls it "a revolt against the forces of cultural uniformity," and at conferences like "Identities versus Globalization," the basic concern is with the protection of local cultures from homogenization.[25] The point, as Franklin Foer, the editor of the *New Republic*, says, is not "to dredge up the tired old Marxist criticisms of capitalism—the big question . . . is less economic than cultural." What Foer worries about is "how people will identify themselves in this new era."

Will "global tastes and brands steamroll indigenous cultures?"
Or will people "revert back to older identities, like religion and
tribe?" He describes himself as surprised by the persistence of
what he pejoratively calls "tribalism" (the tribalism he and
Huntington like is state-sponsored, i.e., nationalism), and suggests that perhaps globalization isn't quite as powerful as we
had supposed it to be.[26] But neither tribalism nor nationalism
is any obstacle to globalization; indeed, they are both fully
compatible with modernization and may even be understood
as two of its most successful products.[27] New forms of "an-
cient" identities are being invented every day. And the function of all of them is to provide people with ways of thinking
about themselves that have as little as possible to do with either
their material circumstances or their political ideals.

So Foer worries about the destruction of indigenous cultures, and some of the indigenous peoples themselves work increasingly hard at maintaining their cultures. Now everybody
wants to stop speaking the language of their oppressor (i.e.,
often, if the oppressor's been the oppressor for long enough, the
language they actually know) and to start speaking the "language of [their] fathers," even if (especially if) the language
wasn't actually spoken by their fathers but was spoken by
someone a little farther back. The choice of fathers, in other
words, and hence the choice of languages, can't be predicated
on proximity; if it were, people would just go on speaking the
languages they actually grew up speaking rather than their
ancestral languages. And even the choice of the right ancestral language is a little fraught. In Brazil, for example, there's
been a revival of a language called Nheengatú, which people

want to establish as an indigenous alternative to Portuguese. The fact that Nheengatú itself (described as a mixture of various Indian, Portuguese and African words) was originally forced upon the native population by Portuguese missionaries, and the further fact that the people now claiming it as their ancestral tongue are not in the main actually descended from the people it was forced upon, are essentially irrelevant. What matters is that it's "a mechanism of ethnic, cultural and linguistic resistance."[28] And the reason that matters is that ethnic, cultural and linguistic resistance is not tired old political or economic resistance. No need to worry about socialism here or the redistribution of wealth. It's the culture, stupid—when the problem is inequality, the solution is identity.

Culture thus does the same kind of work internationally that it does nationally, both economically and ideologically. Economically, it redescribes the material difference between people (I have more, you have less, too bad for you) as cultural difference (I have mine, you have yours, it's all good). It allows us (actually, encourages us) to think that as long as people get to keep on speaking their own languages (and enjoying their own music, not to mention their characteristic foods), there's no reason for alarm. But to see how implausible this is, we have only to imagine ourselves for a second on the losing side of globalization. Imagine the United States fifty years from now— we're so poor that China and India are outsourcing production to the desperate and hence very hardworking masses of Michigan and Ohio. We (the desperate masses) have no unions so we work cheap; we have no health plans so we work sick; we have no retirement plans so we work as long as we possibly

can, which (see "no health plans," above) isn't all that long—
but that's OK because we don't live as long as we used to (or
as the Indians now do). Are we supposed to feel better because
no one's making us speak Mandarin or Hindi? Are we supposed to feel good because, sure we're broke and sick, but at
least we have our culture? Huntington tells us to fight the
"global identity crisis" by remaining American. But when the
crisis part actually involves putting us out of work, it's hard to
see how pride in our identity will do us any good. And it's
even harder to imagine that continuing—against all odds!—
to speak English, we will somehow be resisting globalization.

Of course, the previous paragraph describes a situation that
hasn't yet and may never come about. Even Thomas Friedman,
sounding the alarm about America's potential loss of "power
and influence" if we don't learn to compete better in the global
marketplace, doesn't think we're on the verge of losing our
edge. But it's not as if there aren't costs to winning too, and it's
not as if identity (thinking of yourself as an American rather
than, say, as a worker) doesn't function to obscure them as well.
Many American businesses cannot succeed, Friedman argues
in *The World Is Flat*, without exploiting the "advantages" of
manufacturing in China. The main advantage, of course, is that
the average wage for a factory worker in China is $1,800 a year.
By contrast, the average wage of an American factory worker is
about $54,000 a year, which is not only 3,000 percent higher
than the wage in China but is also 18 percent higher than the
average U.S. salary. In America, factory jobs are good jobs.
And they're also hard to get—factory workers make up only
11 percent of the American workforce. Why? Well, one reason is that in order for America to compete in the global

market, American companies need to do more of their man-ufacturing in China. So even when we're winning, some of us (the ones who no longer work in factories) are losing.[29]

Thus, for example, someone like George Will can (in 2006) accurately describe the American economy as "in the fifth year of a humming expansion,"[30] while it's also true that the pov-erty rate has risen during every year of that expansion. (The most recent figures are 12.7 percent for 2004—up to 37 mil-lion from the 35.9 million it was the year before.) And accord-ing to the *New York Times* writer David Leonhardt, it's not just poor people who have lagged. While sharing Will's view of the economy's performance ("stellar"), Leonhardt points out that "the average hourly wage of rank-and-file workers—a group that makes up 80 percent of the workforce—is slightly lower than it was four years ago."[31] So instead of saying that some of us are losing, I should have said that most of us are losing. Still, as long we think of ourselves as Americans (beating the French, even beating the Chinese), we can be proud. Not only are we speaking English and hanging on to our traditional cultural practices (you may make us play soccer, but you'll never make us watch it), our economy is kicking butt. But, of course, the minute we stop thinking of ourselves as Americans—the min-ute, in other words, we start thinking that the "we" means poor and middle-class people, not Americans, and that the relevant "they" is rich people, not the French or Chinese—things look a little different. What the resisters think of as a struggle to preserve cultural identities and what the advocates think of as a competition between national identities has nothing to do with identities at all.

And in the event that jobs are outsourced to the United

States, there is a final twist: it's not just that our continuing to speak English wouldn't count as a solution; it's that it would count instead as the problem. If we don't learn Hindi, we won't even be able to get the call center jobs that would keep us out of the sweatshops, where all our friends who just speak English work twelve hours a day making athletic shoes to be worn by Asians. (In India, call center jobs are good jobs; wages at Indian call centers are estimated to run between $4,000 and $7,000 a year—that's way higher than in the Chinese factories where my running shoes are made.) So when the United States is going to become the place jobs are outsourced to, I want to be able to speak Hindi or at least make sure that my children do. In a world where economic opportunity depends on the ability to speak Hindi, why would I want them to keep on speaking English? It's not, of course, that Hindi's better than English. As we've seen, no language is better than any other. That's why it's perfectly OK to say in defense of your language what you can't say in defense of your beliefs: you speak it because it's yours. But jobs in call centers *are* better than jobs in sweatshops. And if I want what's best for my kids, don't I want them to speak the language that will get them the best job? Since no language is better than any other, shouldn't I be perfectly happy to see them give up my language?

Those questions, of course, are meant to be rhetorical. The obvious answer is supposed to be "yes." And the reason that answer is supposed to be obvious is that, as we've seen in this chapter, the disappearance of languages is a victimless crime. The disappearance of jobs isn't. Everybody always has a language to speak, and whatever language it is, it's just as good as every other. But not everyone has a job, and not all jobs are equal. So when we focus on globalization as a cultural issue, we're trying to solve a real problem (economic inequality) by working on a false one (cultural identity). If we think that globalization should be resisted, we ought to spend less time worrying about the disappearance of languages and more time worrying about the disappearance of any credible alternative to unfettered capitalism.[32] That is, we need to pay more attention to efforts to invent "new economic models" than to efforts to preserve old cultures. And if we think that globalization can't or shouldn't be resisted, we ought to start learning Hindi. Either way, we shouldn't think that any issue of social justice hangs on the question of which identities, which cultures and which languages survive. Because they're all equal, it doesn't matter which ones survive.

But we can get a sense of how attractive the idea of cultural equality has become and of how successfully it can function to obscure more consequential forms of inequality by recognizing that even in situations where the disappearance of the language would seem to be an unequivocally good thing, some people refuse to let go. Suppose the language you speak is not English but ASL, American Sign Language. You speak it because you're deaf. Like English and Hindi, ASL is neither better nor worse than any other language—you can use it to say everything you need to say—but, like Mati Ke, it may have a problematic future. You, for instance, if you are young enough, might be a good candidate for a cochlear implant and no longer need to speak ASL. Or you and everybody else might have access to a health-care system that radically reduces the chances of your children being born deaf. Indeed, it's precisely insofar as events like this seem to be taking place that scholars like the Australian professor of sign linguistics Trevor Johnston have become increasingly concerned about the possibility of sign's disappearance. Writing in the *American Annals of the Deaf* (the article is called "W(h)ither the Deaf Community?"), Johnston worries that "early implementation of mainstreamed education, free universal access to hearing aids for children under age 18 years, and a federally funded universal health care scheme that subsidizes most of the cost of an initial cochlear implant" are producing a "decline" in the signing deaf community (especially in Australia and the West) that will eventually lead to a "loss of language and culture." "It goes without saying," Johnston remarks, "that this scenario gives me no joy." So even though he himself acknowledges that he may be sounding the alarm prematurely—after all, as he points out, there are still "millions of severely and profoundly deaf children and adults in the underdeveloped and developing world," and, besides, "new and totally unexpected causes for deafness [could] appear tomorrow"—he can't help but feel "deep sorrow" at what he regards as the eventual and "inevitable" "loss of language and culture."[33] The hope for ASL is that inadequate health care and some really catastrophic new diseases could keep it alive for a while longer; the fear is that the cochlear implant and genetic testing will eventually kill it.

But why should anyone be made sorrowful if American and Australian and all the other sign languages disappear? Well, obviously, the disappearance of sign languages would be a bad thing if the people who used them—deaf people—were left without a language. We don't want to lose something useful. But of course the scenario Johnston is predicting is not one in which deaf people are left high and dry while their language dies out; it's one in which the language dies out because there are no more deaf people. So the real cause for sorrow is not the disappearance of a useful language; it's the disappearance of the people who used the language. And at least some people do claim that if deaf people were to disappear, they *would* be sad. Deaf people have a language, as M. J. Bienvenu, the chair of American Sign Language and Deaf Studies at Gallaudet University, reminds us, and they've "got a culture." So "what's wrong with being deaf?" she asks.[34] If the commitment to diversity can make us think we're supposed to be sad when the Mati Ke disappear, why shouldn't we be sad if deaf people disappear too?

This question represents a certain triumph for what is called the "cultural model"—as opposed to the "medical" or "pathological model"—of deafness, and for the effort to get disability in general recognized as "a marker of identity" rather than as a "problem."[35] People who accept the medical model, the Deafness Culture Web site says, are inclined to think of the deaf as "a group . . . whose hearing loss interferes with the normal reception of speech." But people who go for the cultural model are inclined instead to think of them as "a group of persons who share a common language (ASL) and a common culture."[36] From the standpoint of the medical model, the invention of the cochlear implant gets celebrated as a potential cure for deafness; from the standpoint of the cultural model, it gets deplored as at worst a kind of "cultural genocide"[37] and at best a kind of surgical assimilation. I already mentioned the African American novelist George Schuyler's extraordinary satirical novel called *Black No More*, featuring a procedure— the black-no-more procedure—that, as he put it, solved the problem of antiblack prejudice by turning black people white. To those who think of deafness as essentially a culture, the cochlear implant and genetic testing look like versions of the deaf-no-more procedure, more a symptom of the problem than a solution to it.

The alternatives here are a version of the ones we already encountered in thinking about the difference between belonging to an identity group and belonging to an economically defined class. If you think the bad thing about being poor is not that you haven't got any money but the way people treat you because you haven't got any money, you're a victim of classism. If you think the bad thing about being deaf is not that you can't hear but the way people treat you because you can't hear, you're a victim of what gets called "audism" (a neologism created, the Deafness Culture Web site says, on the model of "racism, sexism and anti-semitism"). For those who do believe, however implausibly, that being deaf is having a culture, nothing's wrong with deafness. And this is, of course, what we're being encouraged to think not just about deafness but also about blindness and about the inability to walk when we're being encouraged to put disability alongside race, class and gender on what Simi Linton calls the "diversity agenda." We're being encouraged to think that the problem is the "stigma" placed on disability, not the disability itself. And that the solution is to celebrate diversity instead of stigmatizing it.

But do deaf parents want their children to be deaf like them? Do poor parents want their children to preserve the culture of poverty? The reason the answer to both of these questions is no is that when push comes to shove, all parents understand that hearing and money are not diversity issues, and to think of them as if they were is to substitute a fantasy of equality for the real thing. But even when equality is not a fantasy—as in the case of languages—the commitment to diversity has nothing to do with justice. In fact, it's precisely because different languages (unlike different incomes and unlike different levels of hearing and unlike different ideologies) really *are* equal that no question of social justice rests on their survival. It would be a better world if the descendants of the people who spoke Mati Ke all had access to decent health care and if they all had ways of making a decent living. It would be a better world also if they didn't have silly rules about not talking to their siblings and if, like their counterparts in Bolivia but unlike their counterparts in the United States, they took the resistance to neoliberalism seriously. But it wouldn't be either a better world or a worse one if they still spoke Mati Ke.

6

Religion in Politics: The Good News

If you look at the most recent U.S. Census Bureau publication on poverty in America (it's called *Income, Poverty, and Health Insurance Coverage in the United States: 2004*, and it was issued in August 2005), you will see that the first thing it tells you is that "the number of people in poverty and the poverty rate increased between 2003 and 2004," as did the number of people without health coverage. The second thing it tells you is that "these results were not uniform across demographic groups," and by *demographic groups* it means *races*. The poverty rate overall is 12.7 percent. The rate for blacks is 24.7 percent, and for Hispanics, it's 21.9 percent; whites are at 8.6 percent and Asians at 9.8 percent. Presented in this form—racialized— these numbers are profoundly disturbing, and they are even more profoundly reassuring. They're disturbing because they remind us of the degree to which both the legacy of racism and racism itself are a problem. They're reassuring for what amounts to the same reason. They suggest that people are poor in America today mainly because they are the victims of discrimination, and they thus imply that if we could end discrimination, we could end poverty. But if you look at the statistics a slightly different way, you get a very different story. Of the 37 million poor people in 2004, almost 17 million (45.6 percent of the total) were white. These people are not the victims of discrimination either past or present. And the fact that they aren't is the really disturbing part. We like to think of the American system as essentially fair but marred—as both the right and the left will agree—by racism. But in the case of white people's poverty, the reassurance of the right—that discrimination is a thing of the past—won't help them. And the promises of the left—that they're finally going to wipe discrimination out—won't help them either. Discrimination is not their problem. Diversity is not their solution.[1]

The trouble with diversity, then, is not just that it won't solve the problem of economic inequality; it's that it makes it hard for us even to see the problem. If we're on the right, of course, it's not clear that there is a problem. The right tends to regard economic inequality less as a political issue than as something like a fact of nature—maybe temporary (when free markets triumph, it will go away), maybe permanent (if people make the wrong choices, they have to pay for them), and, either way, not that big a deal (today even poor people have TVs; no one had TVs a hundred years ago). The left, as we have already had occasion to remark, insists on giving poor people identities; it turns them into black people or Latinos or women and treats

them as victims of discrimination as if in a world without discrimination, inequality would disappear. The debate we might
have about inequality thus becomes a debate instead about
prejudice and respect, and—since no one's defending prejudice
and no one's attacking respect—we end up having no debate
at all. And when people do want to have the debate (when they
want to talk about inequality instead of identity), they are criticized by the right as too ideological and by the left as insufficiently sensitive to the importance of race, sex, gender, et
cetera—that is, as too ideological. Hence another version of the
trouble with diversity: it obscures political difference just as
well as it does economic difference. It makes it hard not only
to solve the problem of inequality but even to argue about
whether it is a problem and about what its solution should be.

This obfuscation is what happens when political disagreement gets turned into what the Cincinnati diversity trainer
called "diversity of thought": all thoughts are of equal value;
none is better or worse than any other. In this way, political
belief and affiliation are reconceived along the cultural model,
that is, genuine disagreements are turned into mere differences
in perspective. Indeed, cultural difference has made ideological conflict look like a thing of the Cold War. Ideology's claims
to truth have come to seem irrelevant. This process has been
applied not only to politics but even more vividly to the area
in which the importance of belief should be the most obvious,
religion, and it is in this area that the cultural model is exposed
at its most vacuous. It's one thing, for example, to promote the
virtues of religious tolerance. But it's a very different thing to
celebrate religious diversity ("Theo-diversity," the Global Di-

versity Institute calls it),[2] as if religion too could be transformed into an identity category along the lines of race and culture. Only someone who doesn't believe in any religion can take the view that all religions may plausibly be considered equal and that their differences can be appreciated. From the standpoint of the religions themselves, those differences are a problem, as the claims of both Christianity and Islam to what Pope Benedict XVI calls "universality" make clear. Defending the church against the charge that it is essentially a European institution whose missionary efforts in Africa and elsewhere are attempts to impose European culture, the pope distinguishes between the "false claim to universality on the part of what is simply European" and the core "connection" between salvation and the truth that is "actually universal." Jesus's claim to be "the way, and the truth, and the life," according to the pope, "expresses the basic claim of the Christian faith."[3] Christianity is universal because it is a religion for all peoples (not only Europeans), and it is a religion for all peoples because it tells the "truth."

Like ideological affiliation but more radically, religious identity is very different from racial or cultural identity. The big selling point of cultural identity (the selling point, really, of the very idea of identity) is that cultures are essentially equal. That's what makes them different from classes, since classes are essentially unequal—they involve more or less money. And it makes them different from religions too, since if Christianity tells the truth, all other religions must be false. If you believe that Jesus is the way and I don't believe that Jesus is the way, one of us must be wrong. This is the point that Richard

Neuhaus makes in his influential argument for the relevance of religion to politics, *The Naked Public Square*, when he says that if the Christian view of human history is true, it "is true for everybody, whether they know it or not."[4] As is the Muslim view, the Marxist view, et cetera. Of course, insofar as they contradict each other, they can't all be true; that's what it means to say that there are fundamental disagreements between Christianity and Islam, and even between Catholicism and Protestantism. This is what the pope means when he acknowledges the justice of a Protestant critique of ecumenism which argues that "although they claim to be based on the same Lord, Catholicism and Protestantism are two different ways of understanding and living Christianity," and goes on to insist that "these different ways are not *complementary* but *alternative*."[5] They are alternative instead of complementary because they involve doctrinal differences, differences of belief. Contradictory beliefs cannot be complementary; that's what it means to call them contradictory.

This view of religion understandably makes people of different religions (or no religion) nervous. When Pope Benedict insists on the "connection between salvation and truth" and when he maintains that the relevant truth is that "there is one God . . . Christ Jesus," he isn't leaving much room for those of us who aren't Christian. And he doesn't mean to. In his old Cardinal Ratzinger days, Pope Benedict was known as "God's rottweiler" because of his enthusiastic (and effective) defense of dogma. But his defense of dogma can't be reduced to a mere matter of temperament. If you think that Christianity is a "universal" religion because "it is based on knowledge," you have to think that the alternatives to Christianity are based on lack of knowledge. If you think that Christianity is true, you have to think that everything else isn't. That's why the problem with other Gods is not that they are foreign or malign or weaker but that they are "false."

And, of course, for people whose view of alternative ways to God and beliefs about God is that they *can* be complementary, this is likely to be disconcerting. Indeed, the rise of religious conviction and religious dispute in general has been disconcerting to many. Thus people take comfort in the notion, put forward with special energy by the sociologist of religion Alan Wolfe, that the apparent increase in American religious fervor is essentially nondoctrinal and essentially private. What really matters to most Christians, according to Wolfe, is not "ideas" but "having a personal relationship with Jesus."[6] And the reason this counts as comforting is that it turns religion into a kind of feeling and suggests that differences in belief (about whether, say, homosexuality is a sin) can be transformed into differences of feeling (the difference, say, between your way of having a personal relationship with Jesus and mine).

From the standpoint of the pope, however, and of all those who wish to bring religion back into the public square, it's what people believe rather than how they feel or who they are that matters. Our beliefs are already essentially public in ways that our feelings are not, and they are intrinsically what Neuhaus calls "normative," that is, they have a relation to truth and thus inject us into the public sphere in ways that our identities cannot.[7] If you think abortion is wrong, you think it's wrong not just for you, or for Americans or even for Christians, but for everyone. The conflict between people who believe that abortion is justifiable and people who believe that it is murder is significant precisely because it's not a conflict of identities, but of convictions. Clarence Thomas's race was no doubt essential in getting him nominated to the Supreme Court, but it's his beliefs, not his identity, that have produced his decisions. Indeed, his performance on the bench has been a constant and useful reminder that there is no connection between who you are and what you think; that there is no set of beliefs that goes with being black or white and that as a black (or white or whatever) man, you are not required to have some specific set of beliefs. But, of course, this is completely untrue of religion. There are lots of things that, as a Christian or Muslim or Jew, you *are* required to believe, and if you don't believe them you can't count as a Christian, Muslim or Jew. And since politics to some degree involves your beliefs—you run for office in part by expressing and arguing for them; you govern more or less according to them—it can make no sense to say that religion should be kept out of the public square. If you're running for office and you think God means for you to liberate Iraq, now is the time to mention it.

For the same reason, it makes no sense to complain—as many do—of "prejudice against fundamentalist Christians" or to argue that the old "hatred" of "Jews and blacks" is being refocused as hatred of "the growing evangelical Christian political movement."[8] Thomas Frank, who reports this second remark (made by a *Kansas City Star* columnist John D. Altevogt but widely expressed in more moderate terms by both mainstream conservatives and many liberals), rightly points out the hyperbole involved in describing newspaper attacks on evangelicals as reminiscent (in Altevogt's words) of "the lynch mobs we used to see back when black folks were accused of being too uppity." But the truly bizarre thing here is not so much the exaggeration as it is the redescription of people who have certain beliefs (that Jesus is their savior, that they themselves are born again, etc.) as people who have a certain identity. Fundamentalist Christians are not an ethnic group or a culture. They are people who believe in things like the inerrancy of scripture, the sinfulness of homosexuality, the divinity of Jesus. And if they encounter people who think that all these beliefs are false, what they're encountering is not prejudice but disagreement. Prejudice involves the unjustified assumption that your identity is somehow better than someone else's identity; disagreement involves the absolutely justified—indeed unavoidable—assumption that your belief is better than someone else's belief. (If you didn't think yours was better, you'd give it up.) So we think that Republicans are opposed to Democrats not prejudiced against them; and libertarians aren't prejudiced against socialists, and people who believe in God aren't prejudiced against people who don't. If, as one of the Pew polls suggests, 66 percent of Americans have an "unfavorable" view of atheists, not only is there nothing surprising about that, there's nothing wrong with it.[9] If you are devout, why shouldn't you have an unfavorable view of someone who seems to you profoundly mistaken about what you regard as one of the most fundamental issues of human life?

And the argument obviously works both ways. If you don't believe in God, how can you help but have an "unfavorable" view of all the deeply deluded people who do? That's why when Alan Wolfe says that just as Americans have become "more sensitive to the inequalities of race and gender," they should "extend the same sympathy to those who are different in the sincerity of their belief,"[10] he is missing the point. He is mistaking an inappropriate response to people who seem to us different (prejudice) with an appropriate one to people who seem to us wrong (disagreement). The sympathy we extend to those who have been victimized by prejudice requires us to stop being prejudiced against them; the sympathy we might extend to those who have different beliefs cannot possibly require us to stop thinking they're mistaken. So although it's no doubt true that we shouldn't hate anyone, treating Christians (or atheists) with contempt is not the same as treating black people with contempt; even if we hate Christians (or atheists), we hate them for what they believe, not for who they are. When, in the run-up to John Roberts's confirmation hearings for the Supreme Court, Senator Patrick Leahy declared that we should be as "religious-blind" as we are "color-blind" in considering the qualifications of nominees, he got this exactly wrong.[11] We should be color-blind because color has nothing to do with beliefs. But we shouldn't be religion-blind because religion has everything to do with beliefs. In the public square, the crucial thing about Christians, Muslims, Jews, et cetera, is not whether (like blacks and Asians and women) they're entitled to respect but whether they can convince us that their beliefs are true.

The problem, then, with thinking of religious diversity on the model of cultural diversity is that it turns what should be a debate about the validity of different religious beliefs into a consensus about their equal worth and thus obscures their relevance to public policy. It's precisely religion's claim to universality that makes what Neuhaus calls "religiously based public values" matter in American political life. By *public*, he means first that the religious component should not be privatized; we can't think of someone's faith the way Jefferson famously did when he remarked that "it does me no injury for my neighbor to say there are twenty gods or no God. It neither picks my pocket nor breaks my leg." If my neighbor's belief in God involves also, say, a belief that abortion is wrong, it does and it ought to affect me. It cannot be treated as a merely private fact about him, such as the fact that he likes Chinese food or opera. And by *public*, Neuhaus also means that the religious arguments made in the public or political sphere should themselves be what he calls "transsubjective." "Public decisions," he says, "must be made by arguments that are public in character. A public argument is transsubjective. It is not derived from sources of revelation or disposition that are essentially private and arbitrary."[12] Identities can be private—it really does do me no injury if my neighbor is black. Identities are not transsubjective—the things that make me who I am need not make anybody else who she is. But beliefs, Neuhaus rightly insists, are neither.

There is, however, a certain tension between these two senses of the public, between the requirement that we recognize the public claims of religious belief and the requirement that those claims not be "derived" from "private" sources like "revelation." The difficulty is in preserving the religious base of the values in question while meeting the criteria that enable them to go public. Suppose we take two political issues that today have an undeniable public importance and that are often linked to religious convictions: abortion and gay marriage. What contribution does religion have to make to the debate over these issues? The argument against abortion is that it is murder, and you don't need to be a Christian or, for that matter, to have any religious convictions at all to think that murder is wrong. Indeed, almost all the people who support abortion, including atheists, oppose murder but deny that abortion is murder, insisting that the fetus does not yet count as a person (and thus cannot be murdered) or that the pregnant woman's refusal to accept the unchosen obligation to bear the child does not meet the legal definition of murder. So what the opponents of abortion need to do is show these people that they are mistaken, that the fetus does count as a person. How does religion help? Why, for example, should the fact that most Protestant evangelical churches and the Catholic Church oppose abortion count as a reason for people who don't oppose abortion to change their minds? How does telling people that God doesn't want them to do it make a difference if the people you're telling don't believe in God?

The problem here is that the specifically religious part of the argument is entirely (to use Neuhaus's terms) "private and arbitrary," dependent on "revelation" in a way that the conviction that we can't draw a sharp line between the fetus and a person is not. If I am trying to convince you that the fetus is a person, I can—to take a standard argument—point out that if you don't regard the fetus as a person, you won't be able to regard people in comas as persons either, since they are similarly unconscious, dependent on others, et cetera. And you may be led to reflect that the considerations that cause you to think it's wrong to pull the plug on people in comas (they may recover consciousness; they may once again come to function as persons) are applicable to the unborn child as well: if nurtured, it too will come to be a person. So you may decide that you were mistaken in distinguishing so sharply between the fetus and a person, and you may come to believe that abortion is wrong. Or you may not. For our purposes here, it doesn't matter how we come out on the abortion debate; what matters is just that we recognize how limited is the role that religious conviction plays in that debate.

For consider the alternative, the idea that in convincing you that abortion is wrong, I'm convincing you not simply to alter your values but somehow to take into account the importance of their being religiously based. What this means is that not only do I have to convince you; I have to convert you. I have to get you to believe not only that abortion is wrong but that it's wrong because God forbids it. Which is to say, I have to get you to believe in God. And here it's notoriously the case that arguments of the sort that might conceivably prevail in the public square will be of very little use. How many people get argued into a belief in God? And why should people who don't believe in God, or don't believe in your God, be the slightest bit impressed by your insistence that (your) God forbids abortion? Or that your God is against gay marriage?

The gay marriage example is actually a sharper one because it's so different. The strength of the antiabortion argument is its appeal to our intuition that murder is wrong, an intuition we have no problem fleshing out with considerations involving our own desires not to be ourselves the victims of murder and not to have our loved ones be the victims of murder. But it's a lot harder to come up with equally plausible intuitions about homosexuality; it's a lot harder to see how anyone is victimized by homosexuality. No doubt, this is why being anti-gay often seems like a kind of prejudice—more like being anti-Semitic, say, than like being anti-Republican. If, however, you think that homosexuality is wrong, it's hard to see how you can be accused of prejudice against gays, just as it's hard to see how people who think that fundamentalists are wrong can be accused of being prejudiced against them. Disapproval of what people do doesn't count as prejudice any more than disagreement with what people believe. So the good news for homophobes is that they're not bigots; they believe that homosexuality is wrong, and they have their reasons. But the bad news is that their reasons are so weak. Because while it's easy to see that homosexuality is bad if it goes against the laws of God, it's really hard to see much wrong with it if it doesn't go against the laws of God or if we don't believe there are any such things as the laws of God. So while the arguments against abortion don't rely on religious belief, the arguments against gay marriage seem to rely on almost nothing but religious belief. It says in Leviticus 18:22, "Thou shalt not lie with mankind, as with womankind: it is abomination." Other things Leviticus tells you not to do include trimming the corners of your beard (21:5), wearing clothes made of linen "mingled" with wool (19:19) and sleeping with your wife (much less anyone else's wife) while she's being "put apart for her uncleanness" (18:19). Neuhaus says that "when asked why certain attitudes or behavior is right or wrong, the great majority of Americans answer that the Bible or the church or religious teaching says it is so."[13] But almost no Americans believe that trimming your beard at the corners is wrong despite the fact that the Bible says it is. And if homosexuality is wrong only in the way that trimming the corners of your beard is wrong, why should Americans be against it?

But it's not the inconsistency that's the problem here. Even though the degree to which literalist readers of scripture feel free to pick and choose the bits they're obligated to obey and the bits they're not is pretty impressive, the real problem is the appeal to nothing but God's stated prohibition. This doesn't mean that you shouldn't be allowed to make the appeal. It doesn't mean that people who really do believe Leviticus can't cite it. It just means that it's hard to see why the rest of us should heed them. Neuhaus says that if "we witness a son who routinely abuses his aged mother, we know that it is wrong," and that if we're asked to give our reasons, "most Americans would likely invoke biblical injunctions about the honor due parents." But, he complains, "according to current doctrine, that reason is not publicly admissible."[14] Well, it obviously is publicly admissible, but, depending on who the public is, it may not be very convincing. The force of examples like the ones from Leviticus is that many of us (even those of us who believe the Bible is divinely inspired) don't feel a moral obligation to do things just because the Bible tells us to. If we think the son abusing his aged mother is doing wrong, we have reasons in addition to or utterly separate from the fact that the Bible says it is.

People who think you shouldn't trim the corners of your beard have every right to try to convince others that they shouldn't either. They even have every right to try to pass laws forbidding the trimming. It's no doubt true that such laws would be unconstitutional, but the fact that something isn't constitutional doesn't in itself make it wrong. Slavery was constitutional but wrong, which was what Supreme Court Justice Thurgood Marshall had in mind when in his famous speech on the bicentennial of the U.S. Constitution, he described it as a document that was "defective from the start." And the effort today to imagine that all the things we think are good should be at worst allowed by and at best actually mandated by the Constitution is, despite its popularity, implausible on its face. Some of the strategies for the enforcement of equal opportunity that I myself would like to see enacted in the United States (e.g., the abolition of private schools) are almost certainly not constitutional. In other words, this is not a point about the separation of church and state. It's a point about the limitations of the appeal to divine revelation as an argument: if the people you're arguing with already believe in the revelation, you don't need the argument; if they don't, the argument can't possibly convince them.

Because Christianity importantly (if not exclusively) consists in a set of beliefs about public issues, it must have a role to play on the public square. But because many of its beliefs seem so false to so many, we ought to seek to constrain that role—not by ruling the appeal to religion out of court but by objecting to the false things the religious may say. So if one reason we want to keep the Ten Commandments out of our courtrooms is to prevent the establishment of Christianity as a state religion, another reason is that many of us don't believe them. The point about the Ten Commandments, as Neuhaus reminds us, is that they are commandments; "They are not, as it has been said, Ten Suggestions or Ten Significant Moral Insights, to be more or less appreciated according to one's subjective disposition."[15] What it means to be a believer in the Ten Commandments is to believe that it is in fact wrong to do the things they enjoin against, and that anybody who does not believe in the Ten Commandments is mistaken, and that anyone who does not follow them is behaving wrongly. But it's for this very reason that unbelievers will find their presence in the courtroom obnoxious. They think the claim ("I am the Lord thy God") that authorizes the first one ("thou shalt not have other gods before me") is false and that therefore none of the first four commandments (no graven images, etc.) needs to be followed. Number five—"Honor thy Father and Mother"—has a different kind of force, precisely, as we already noted, because it does not depend on believing in the Lord, our God, but we may or may not think it's a good idea and, more to the point, we may believe it's a bad one and act on our belief without breaking the laws of the state. Numbers six through nine are like number five in that our belief in them need not hinge on our feelings about the Lord, but they are stronger than five because they are not only things that Christians should and shouldn't do; they are things that, broadly speaking, no one should do. And number ten is kind of ambiguous, depending on what we think is meant by *covet*.

So if you're an unbeliever, the problem with the Ten

Commandments—correctly bearing in mind what Neuhaus calls their "normative status"—is that four of them are false. And when I say they're false, I don't mean that they're not true for me or that they don't make an impact on what Neuhaus calls my "subjective disposition." Although the preferred target of people who argue for the importance of religion in our lives is relativism—the idea that there are different truths for different people—it should be obvious that the argument I am making here has nothing to do with this idea. The clarifying thing about religious disputes—the thing that distinguishes conflicts of belief from the conflicts of identity in which nationalists and multiculturalists have so much invested—is that the conflicts of belief are precisely not relativized. When I say that four of the ten commandments are not true, I mean that they're not true for me or for anyone else and that the people who think they are true—who think that they are being told to, say, keep the Sabbath by the Lord their God—are mistaken. Those who defend the significance of religion in daily life are right to argue that, as Neuhaus puts it, "even if one is not a believer, the divorce of public business from the moral vitalities of the society is not desirable."[16] But the identification of "moral vitalities" with the belief in supernatural entities issuing instructions from above is not such a good idea either.

My main point here is not, however, that religious beliefs are mistaken. It is instead that disputes about religion—understood as the pope understands them, as disputes about what is universally true—are useful reminders that you can't exactly be for diversity of beliefs in the way that you can be for diversity of identities. We encourage diversity of belief in the hope that having lots of different ideas will help us figure out which ones are true. So ideological diversity is valuable not in itself but instrumentally. But no one thinks the point of encouraging different identities is to help us decide which ones are the best. Just the opposite; they're all good. When it comes to cultural identity, it's the diversity itself, not the thing the diversity leads to, that we're supposed to like.

The trouble with diversity, from this perspective, is that it tries to imagine a world in which no one is a believer, as if even our belief in God (or our belief that there is no God) were just another aspect of our identity. But belief is at the heart of both our religion and politics, and insofar as the displacement of ideology by identity has helped bring religious beliefs to the fore, it cannot possibly make sense to keep pretending that the best way to deal with them is by asserting that religion has no place in politics. It has a lot more place in politics than race and culture do. It "is not so unthinkable," Neuhaus reminds us, "that people should be willing to kill and be killed for religion."[17] One reason it's not so unthinkable is, of course, that it has often happened. The more important reason, however, is that fighting for your religion involves fighting for something you believe in, for something you think is better than what you're fighting against. The point can be made more obvious by being made less melodramatic. Forget killing and being killed; go with arguing. You can't even get the argument started unless you understand that the relevant difference between you and the other party is not the difference in identity but the difference in beliefs, and that what the argument is about is whose beliefs are better.

Another way to put this is to say that the debate over whether America should or shouldn't be Christian is a lot more worthwhile than the debate over whether it should or shouldn't remain American. In fact, it's hard even to have a debate when it's about identity. What are we arguing about when we're arguing over whether the "Star-Spangled Banner" should be sung only in English? There are real issues involved in the current controversy over immigration—issues having to do with the insourcing of labor and with the possibility of organizing workers internationally—but the question of whether or not you're declaring your loyalty to the United States if you don't declare it in English isn't one of them.

While the debate over whether America should be Christian is a step in the right direction, a debate over whether America should continue to worship at the altar of the free market would be better still. The last election almost completely avoided the subject, and both the war on terrorism and the red state/blue state issues whose corporate utility Thomas Frank so convincingly describes have helped us continue to avoid it. Indeed, even the war in Iraq has functioned as a distraction, since opposition to the Bush administration's criminally reckless foreign policy has taken pride of place over opposition to its at least equally destructive domestic policy. Although it's not like the Democrats have been on the front lines for equality either, even though John Edwards's Two Americas stump speech in the 2002 campaign was a real sign of progress.

What made it so was that its two Americas were not racial or cultural but rich and poor, and the fact that they have grown even farther apart since that election has begun to make the irrelevance of identity even more vivid. Maybe it will make the relevance of ideology—the importance of our beliefs— more vivid too. People sometimes say that economic and ideological issues put voters off. But almost half the population already doesn't vote. And most of the nonvoters are poor. It would be interesting to see how many of them would start showing up for elections that hinged on the meaning and importance of equality in America.

Conclusion: About the Author

Walter Benn Michaels teaches at the University of Illinois, Chicago. He makes $175,000 a year. But he wants more; one of his motives for writing this book was the cash advance offered him by his publishers. Some readers will be tempted to see a discrepancy between these facts and the arguments against economic inequality made in the preceding chapters. But they should remember that those arguments are true (if they are true) even if Michaels's motives are bad, and they would be false (if they were false) even if his motives were good. Not to put too fine a point on it, the validity of the arguments does not depend on the virtue of the person making them. Furthermore, the point of the book is not that people, including its author, should be virtuous. During the summer in which most of this book was written, a homeless man lived in the railroad underpass Michaels can see out his study window. A more virtuous person might have been at least tempted to go down and bring him some breakfast or maybe even invite him in for a shower and a meal. It never occurred to Michaels to do either of these things. Mainly he wished the man would go away. And his desire for the man to just not be there does not contradict the argument of this book; it's more like the motive for the argument of this book. The point is not that we should be nicer to the homeless; it's that no one should be homeless.

The fact that Michaels makes $175,000 a year puts him in the top 3 percent of the American population. The fact that his total household income is more like $250,000 a year almost gets him into the top 1 percent. And maybe the money earned through writing this book will push him over the line—top 1 percent![1] What this means is that he is not a member of the middle class. He is a member of the upper middle class. Comparatively few people are richer than he is. And, yet, he finds this very hard to believe. He does not feel rich. Why not? Well, for one thing, he is confronted on a daily basis by the spectacle of people who are much richer than he is. For example, like many members of the upper middle class, he is a daily reader of the *New York Times,* and one of the primary functions the *Times* performs for its upper-middle-class readers is to make them feel poorer. It does this by publishing articles like "Is $200,000 the New $100,000?" or articles about the difference in status between people who have the nanny pick the children up after school and people who bring the nanny along with them when they themselves pick the children up. (If you send the nanny in your place, it shows you haven't got the time to do the job yourself but you do have the money to pay someone to do it for you; if you bring the nanny with you, it shows you have the time but you're so rich you're prepared to pay anyway—you win.)[2] Reading these stories, Michaels experiences the standard mixture of envy and disapproval, but what he experiences above all is a deeply legitimating disidentification. *He* could never afford to do that! His household may be in the top 2 or 3 percent, but his $250,000 a year puts him a lot closer to the median of $44,389 than to the people who bring the nanny or to the people who send her.

Why is this disidentification legitimating? Because it leads Walter Benn Michaels to think of himself as *not* rich; it leads him to think that when he talks about the problem of economic inequality, he is not the problem, the superrich are. And, of course, the superrich *are* part of the problem. But, unfortunately, he is too. Compared to the superrich, he may feel poor, but feeling poor doesn't make you poor. And, even more to the point, feeling rich doesn't make you rich. Many polls show that Americans characteristically think of themselves either as already having moved up in class (the *Times* reported that 45 percent identified themselves as belonging to a higher social class as adults than they did as children) or as being about to move up in class. In 1996, slightly under two thirds of Americans (64 percent) between the ages of eighteen and twenty-nine thought that it was either very likely or somewhat likely that they would become rich—they defined *rich* as making $100,000 a year.[3] It's ten years later, and they aren't there yet. The median per capita income is much less than half that, and the share of the population making $100,000 is only about 7 percent. Of course this particular cohort still has some time left, but the fact remains: in a society where only about 7 percent of the population makes $100,000 a year, the anticipation by 64 percent of that population that it will join the 7 percent is profoundly mistaken. Young people in America have about as realistic an assessment of their economic situations as, say, the contestants on *American Idol* have of their singing ability.

Indeed, *American Idol* (the most watched show among people twenty-five and younger) is a kind of emblem of our fantasies about success, and the popularity of the show is a function of its ability to portray us to ourselves. Although, as in any tournament, only one person will win, the system the show embodies is in a certain sense absolutely fair: every contestant has a chance to win, and to take your chance, all you have to do is try out. So there's a kind of formal equality of opportunity among the contestants. But that formal equality is not, from a statistical standpoint, very encouraging since, when there are over 100,000 people auditioning for the contest, your individual chance of winning looks very small. So this is where what one critic has called the "delusional self-confidence" of the participants kicks in. If you start factoring in your talent and your hard work and the intensity of your commitment to "following your dream" (a phrase that at this moment in American history appears to have almost talismanic power), you can find yourself thinking you've got a real shot. And sometimes it's not till you actually get yourself on TV that someone (the English guy) makes it clear that in fact you have no talent and no chance whatsoever. So what the show presents is both a vision of the world in which the truly talented will succeed (the American dream!) and a vision of the high level of self-deception—I'm talented! I will succeed!—required to live happily in that world (the American delusion).

This use of the word *delusion* may be unfair. When Bruce Bartlett (respected conservative economist, formerly a senior fellow with the National Center for Policy Analysis and former Deputy Assistant Director for Economic Policy in the Treasury Department) looks at the same data Michaels has been looking at—data showing that the belief in upward mobility has increased as the reality of upward mobility has decreased—he comes up with a very different conclusion. Bartlett says that although the actual numbers show class mobility in America to be declining, "the ranks of the middle and upper middle classes have increased." The evidence for this conclusion is that, when asked about their class position, "only 28 percent of people reported growing up middle [class], and just 8 percent said they had lived in an upper-middle class home." But today, "42 percent of people say they belong to the middle class and 15 percent are part of the upper middle class." So there's a 14 percent increase in the middle class and a 7 percent increase in the upper middle class, and "there is no evidence whatsoever of economic class stagnation or deterioration."[4]

Bartlett's idea here is not that these numbers match up with actual changes in income; everyone agrees that they don't. His idea is that class and class mobility are functions of how people feel about their position. It's like the OMB's account of "self-perception" in the reporting of ethnic status for the census. The economic data, Bartlett says, "are unambiguous because people are reporting their relative position as they see it. And in this case, perception is reality."[5] So where OMB says that you belong to whatever *race* you perceive yourself as belonging to, Bartlett thinks you belong to whatever *class* you perceive yourself as belonging to. The liberal account of race as a social construction is matched by the conservative account of class as a social construction. Liberals think your race is whatever you believe it is; conservatives think your class is whatever you believe it is. The idea in both cases is that in America you can be whatever you want to be—the American dream!

So although you don't get to be rich by thinking of yourself as rich, it turns out that—at least from Bartlett's point of view—you do. As long as you think you're middle class, you are middle class; believing makes it so. Indeed, not only can poor people get richer by just believing, rich people can get poorer too. When a man making $130,000 a year sums up his economic achievement by saying, "I'm in the middle and I'm happy,"[6] he is at best only half right. He's actually closer to the ninety-fifth percentile in income, nowhere near the middle. We know what he means, of course: he doesn't feel rich. He sees lots of people richer than he is, both in reality and in the newspapers and, especially, on TV. And just as the black kids on campus make the white kids feel better about themselves, so do the superrich make the merely rich feel better. In fact, the social construction of class is even more useful than the social construction of race, since the social construction of race just enables you to ignore the difference between the rich and the poor while the social construction of class makes it possible to eliminate it. If you really can convince yourself that people belong to whatever class they think they belong to and if you can get everybody (the rich and the poor) to think they belong to the middle class, then you've accomplished the magical trick of redistributing wealth without actually transferring any money. Marx used to describe religion as the opium of the people because it promised them in heaven what they couldn't get on earth. The American dream is more effective; it assures us that we don't have to wait for the afterlife. The poor already have what they haven't got, and the rich don't really have what they do. Everybody's happy.

◆

So Walter Benn Michaels is quite rich even if he doesn't feel he is. That's his class. But what about his culture, his identity? For Walter Benn Michaels is not only upper middle class, he is also Jewish. God only knows what he means when he writes this, but, since he doesn't believe in God, it doesn't mean he believes in or practices Judaism. And it also doesn't mean he believes in the existence of a Jewish race or of a Jewish culture that could be somehow defined without reference to either race or religion. The problem with the Jewish race idea is, as biologist Robert Pollack puts it, "there are no DNA sequences common to all Jews and absent from all non-Jews. There is nothing in the human genome that makes or diagnoses a person as a Jew."[7] And even if there were some such sequences, there would be nothing that followed from them, nothing that counted as what we mean by an identity. Furthermore, the kinds of things we ordinarily mean by cultural heritage aren't really available either. No doubt, many of Michaels's ancestors spoke Yiddish; this does not produce in him the sense that he ought to speak Yiddish too. Some of them seem to have been farmers, but he doesn't find himself looking longingly past the Chicago suburbs toward the fertile plains. Some of the things he does are stereotypically associated with Jews (he likes lox and bagels; he uses his hands a lot when he talks; he wants to make more money). Most of the things he does are not. But even the stereotypical ones are not *constitutive* of Jewishness (you don't have to be Jewish to like lox and bagels, you for sure don't have to be Jewish to want to make more money)—so if his DNA can't make him Jewish, neither can his culture. If he were to undergo the genetic testing that has recently become popular, he would no doubt find that some percentage of his ancestors came from somewhere and some other percentage came from somewhere else. Everybody comes from somewhere. He might also get some potentially useful information about his health. But what he wouldn't get—what no one ever gets— is an identity, a culture.

♦

The description of the author as Jewish, then, doesn't really tell you very much, certainly not as much as the $175,000 a year salary or the fact that he's a professor. And not only a professor but a professor of English, which means that he's been at the heart of the culture wars since he started earning a paycheck. University English departments have, over the last twenty years, developed a reputation for being hotbeds of radicalism. Indeed, as the academic generation to which Michaels belongs got promoted, conservatives started mockingly referring to them as tenured radicals, and sometimes they, not so mockingly, referred to *themselves* as tenured radicals. The content of their supposed radicalism was the insistence on race, gender, and class as fundamental categories of literary analysis, and the reason this looked radical to their right-wing critics is that it seemed to politicize great works of literature and to judge them not on their literary merit but on how well they matched current liberal standards of ethical behavior. (Truth in packaging: Michaels himself has written a book, *Our America,* arguing that American literature of the 1920s cannot be correctly understood without understanding the racial commitments it embodied.) Thus the right thinks university English departments (and humanities departments more generally) are radical because they castigate dead white males and foreground the roles of the nonwhite, of women, and of the gay, the lesbian and the transgendered. And the English departments themselves, understanding perfectly well that this is a caricature, nevertheless try to push the envelope even farther, adding, say, the disabled to the identity categories above and thinking of themselves as more truly radical for doing so.

But they are both wrong. There is nothing politically radical about insisting on and even celebrating diversity; on the contrary, celebrating diversity, as this book has argued, is now our way of accepting inequality. This is why it's a mistake to believe that the humanities departments of our universities are hotbeds of leftism, even though both the supposedly left-wing professors and their right-wing critics love to believe it. In fact, they're more like the research and development division of neo-liberalism. The more kinds of difference they can come up with to appreciate (not just many races but mixed races, not just gay and lesbian but gay, lesbian, bisexual and transgendered), the more invisible becomes the difference that a truly left politics would want to eliminate: class difference.

Which is why class has always seemed a little like the odd man out in the race/gender/class trinity—it's not as if the academic left wants to get rid of race and gender. But this contradiction has been pretty effectively solved by turning class into class identification, and thereby making it respectable too. The trick here is to stop worrying about how much money people actually have and concentrate instead on almost everything else about them. Thus the historian John Womack has brilliantly described the new historians of the working class as interested in everything about the working class—its racial and cultural and sexual identifications—except its work.[8] And Michaels's own field, literary criticism, has made its particular contribution by beginning to study the literature of the working class in the same way that it now studies African American or Asian American literature. What this does is turn class position into culture, something—like heritage—to be proud of after all. But why should the fact of poverty be a point of pride or a badge of authenticity? And why should professors of literature be committed to appreciating the poetry of the poor? Or to thinking that it counts as a blow for justice when they do? If you are committed to equality, that commitment is—must be—based on the idea that those who have been denied equality have been deprived. And the commitment to the poor is based precisely on the sense that they are deprived, that they are victims. But once we start insisting that working-class literature has its own value and that, as literary critics, we have done the poor an injustice by failing to appreciate their literature—you commit yourself not only to ignoring but to erasing the inequality, not by removing the deprivation but by denying that it is deprivation.

My point here is not that working class or poor people can't produce great literature but that they do so only by overcoming an obstacle, the obstacle of being working class or poor. Denying that poverty is an obstacle—treating working-class literature on the model of, say, French literature—denies the relevance of class inequality. From this perspective, the idea that teachers of literature should be committed to what one critic calls "valuing" "working-class cultures" is fundamentally reactionary.[9] Indeed, the minute you start reading literature by poor people in the same way you read ethnic literatures, you've arrived in something like inequality heaven. Where you used to just distract yourself from economic difference by focusing on cultural difference, now you can celebrate economic difference by pretending that it *is* cultural difference.

And this trick works for rich people as well as for poor people. When a social critic like Michael Lind says that the differences between what he calls the "over class" and the middle class should not be understood in terms of "income categories" but in terms of "fashions and folkways," he's gotten the hang of it even though he's not a professor. The over class "eats pâté and cheese," Lind says; the middle class "eats peanut butter and Velveeta"; the over class "plays squash and tennis," "the middle class plays pool and bowls." If you watch public television and are "saving for a vacation in Rome or Paris," you belong to the over class "even if your salary is not very impressive"; if you watch the Nashville Network and are saving for a vacation in Las Vegas, you don't—"no matter how much money you make."[10]

It is true that accounts of class ought to be more sophisticated than mere facts about wealth and income, and although the Velveeta-versus-imported-cheese opposition is a little crude, it's clear what Lind is saying: even if they haven't got much money, people who know the difference between a good Stilton and a bad one may well think of themselves (and even be thought of by others) as in some sense superior to people who don't. And, by the same token, people with a great deal of money may well think of themselves (and be thought of by others) as regular guys—if they just stay off the squash court (or avoid windsurfing). But from the standpoint of economic fairness, what does it matter whether you spend your money in Paris or Las Vegas? Exactly what injustice are rich Velveeta eaters enduring? Lind is thinking that the people who go to Paris look down on the ones who go to Las Vegas, and probably they do. But so what? It may be unpleasant to have people think they're better than you but it's not unfair. The unfairness is not in people making fun of your choices; the unfairness is in your not getting to make those choices.

Walter Benn Michaels doesn't eat Velveeta. Walter Benn Michaels would rather go to Paris. He thinks that some people have better taste than others, and he thinks he is one of those people. The point of this book is not that no one should ever feel superior to anyone else or even that no one really is superior to anyone else. Just the opposite: in taste as in class there is better and worse. Of course, it hardly matters whether we treat tastes as equal. But treating classes as if they are too is one of our most effective ways of ignoring an inequality that does matter. When it comes to economic inequality, we should stop finding ways to ignore it, we should concentrate not on respecting the illusions of cultural difference but on reducing the reality of economic difference. That is the heart of a progressive politics.

Afterword to the 2016 Edition

This afterword is being written in September 2015, almost exactly ten years after I finished the book that precedes it and, in terms of diversity, a lot has happened. In a development I definitely did not see coming, we elected and then reelected our first African American president. Almost as surprising, where in 2005 only one state (Massachusetts) allowed same-sex marriage, now it's the constitutional right of every American. Much less surprising, the foreign-born population of the United States has increased from 35.16 million to (an all-time high) 41.3 million,[1] and the percentage of the population that is white has dropped from 67 percent to 62.2 percent. So today we live in a country that is even more diverse than it was ten years ago and that, in important ways, is also more committed to ending some of the discriminatory practices that ten years ago seemed pretty firmly in place. When, for example, diversity training comes to include instructions for asking people what their preferred pronouns are (he? she? hir? ze? they?), progress has been made.

Which is not to say that there hasn't been opposition. Some people are bizarrely outraged by the genderqueer (which bathroom will ze use?). Many more were obviously unnerved by the election of a black president with unexceptional pronouns but an African name (as of this writing the highest-polling Republican candidate for president is still questioning whether Barack Obama was born in the United States) and many others have attacked the president in unmistakably racist terms. And the increase in immigration—and hence ethnic diversity—has produced compensatory fantasies about building a wall between the U.S. and Mexico and even Canada.

But immigration continues apace, and it's supported not just by liberals who see opposition to it as a form of racism but by many conservatives who see opposition to it as a threat to profits. From the late nineteenth century, when Italian immigrants fresh off the boat were used as scabs against (mainly white) striking Pennsylvania coal miners, to the early twenty-first century, when Mexican immigrants have been brought in to displace (mainly black) farmworkers in the Vidalia, Georgia onion fields, American employers have understood the value of cheap labor. The nineteenth-century miners expressed their skepticism about workforce diversity by fighting a pitched battle against the immigrants and killing seven of them; the more law-abiding twenty-first-century farm workers went to court, alleging they'd been "fired because of their race and national origin."[2] To which their employers replied that they had nothing against black, white or American workers; it's just that "When José gets on the bus to come here from Mexico he is committed to the work. . . . He leaves his family at home. The work is hard, but he's ready. A domestic (i.e. born in America) wants to know: What's the pay? What are the conditions? In these communities, I am sorry to say, there are no fathers at home, no role models for hard work. They want rewards without input."

By which they meant that domestics are not satisfied with the forty cents they get for each five-pound bucket of onions they pick.[3]

Of course the farmers' complaint that Americans don't work hard enough because they were brought up without fathers is a little hard to swallow (is "José" at home with his kids in Mexico?), but the relevant point is that the employers' commitment to diversity and to cheap labor are indistinguishable. Which is why both liberal and conservative economists have almost always supported lots of legal immigration and why some of them even speak approvingly of illegal immigration (because it responds fastest to market forces; illegals come when there's the possibility of jobs; they leave when those jobs dry up). The advantage of the immigrants is that, unlike the domestics, they're too desperate to ask, "What's the pay? What are the conditions?"

And that's good for employers because, unsurprisingly, as diversity has flourished, the pay and the conditions have only gotten worse. The subtitle of this book is *How We Learned to Love Identity and Ignore Inequality*. Since the Great Recession (2007–2009), it's no longer exactly true that we ignore economic inequality, and the Occupy movement certainly drew our attention to the difference between the 1 percent and the 99 percent. But neither Occupy nor anyone else has managed to do anything about reducing that difference. Since 2005, the poor have gotten poorer. In 2005, if you were in the twentieth percentile, you were making $21,668; in 2013, you were making $20,885. The rich have gotten richer: the ninetieth percentile went from $142,288 to $150,000.[4] And the very rich are much richer; in fact, in recent years, while the average income of the bottom 99 percent has fallen (by 0.4 percent), the average of the 1 percent rose by 36.8 percent (to $1,303,198).[5]

Furthermore, as economic inequality rises, so does the enthusiasm for addressing every other, *non*-economic kind of inequality. Everyone knows that the whole point of working on Wall Street is to make lots of money: in 2014, while the median salary for U.S. workers was about $53,000, the average bonus on Wall Street was $172,860. (And that's just the bonus; the average base pay was $355,900.)[6] But probably not everyone realizes just how committed Wall Street is to diversity. Goldman Sachs, for example, has (among many other honors) been named a Stone Wall Star Performer (for consistently demonstrating exemplary practices to support lesbian, gay and bisexual staff), a Best Company for Multicultural Woman and the Overall Best Employer for Asian Pacific Americas Professionals. And when it comes to sexual reassignment (as opposed to income redistribution), Wall Street and what's left of Occupy Wall Street (essentially a Web site and a twitter feed) share values that run at least as deep as their differences: Occupy celebrates Carrie Davis becoming the first transgender person to win a "Woman of Distinction" Award from the state of New York, while Citigroup, Credit Suisse and, of course, Goldman win plaudits for offering their employees insurance that will help pay for treatments and procedures "related to gender transition or sex reassignment."

But it's not just Wall Street that embraces both inequality and diversity. Gary Becker, the conservative Nobel Prize–winning economist disapproved of what he thought of as the bad inequality produced by discrimination just as fervently as he approved of the good kind produced by markets. The "inequality in earnings" that labor markets produced was "mainly the good kind,"[7] rewarding hard work and ability, while the inequality produced by racism, is not only morally wrong but also, he argued in his first book (*The Economics of Discrimination*) bad for capitalism, and especially for capitalists. Why? In competitive markets employers can't afford to indulge what he called the "taste" for discrimination, a preference for one racial group over another—they need to be able to get people who will work as hard as possible for as little as possible. Which is why those Georgia onion farmers want to hire Mexicans. If they could afford to indulge their real racial "taste," they might want to hire white people like themselves. But if they want to keep the costs of labor as low as possible, even the most racist employers can't afford their racism, they can't afford arbitrarily to constrict their labor pool. So as fathers and husbands, even as voters and taxpayers, they may well be prejudiced against both Mexicans and blacks but, as employers, they're extremely eager to hire the cheapest and most frightened.

Of course, this doesn't mean that discrimination in hiring

or race- and gender-based gaps in earnings have disappeared. (The most recent numbers, for 2013, tell us that Asian men make the most money and Hispanic women make the least. After the Asian men come white men, and after white men, Asian women.[8]) What it does mean is that in the ideal world imagined by today's economic orthodoxy, inequalities based in race and gender would disappear—no worker would make more than another because of his race. But inequalities determined by the market would not; no worker would make more than the lowest salary her employer could get her to work for. And the same anti-discriminatory principles would apply to people hoping to be on the higher end of the wage scale or even to be employers themselves. In other words, it's not income inequality that's the problem; it's the kind of inequality that was produced the wrong way—through racism or sexism.

Our concern with the wrong kind of inequality explains why we care so much about who goes to college. Among adults between the ages of 25 and 32, those with four-year degrees or higher earn $17,500 more than people who didn't go to college at all and $15,500 more than people who graduated from two-year programs (Pew), and the gap only increases as people get older. So it's important that underrepresented minorities stop being underrepresented, and that's been the goal of the race-based affirmative action programs that have been one of the several techniques used to make college students a more diverse group. Today, if you're reading this for a class in a four-year college, there's a little over 60 percent chance that you're non-Hispanic white, about 12 percent that you're black,

10 percent that you're Hispanic and 6 percent that you're Asian. These numbers don't exactly match the U.S. population but, except for the underrepresentation of Latinos, they come pretty close. And if you're at an elite school, the diversity will be even greater. In the Harvard class of 2019, for example, Latinos are at 12.5 percent, blacks at 11.2 percent and whites are down to 58 percent while Asians are up to 30 percent. In terms of race, a school like Harvard is approaching the minority-majority nation that demographers say American children under the age of five have already begun to live in.

But in terms of class, as we already know, it's going in exactly the opposite direction. Over half of Harvard's students come from families making more than $125,000 a year and almost a third from families making more than $250,000 a year. Only 4 percent come from the bottom quintile. The number of minority students, in other words, is about ten times the number of poor students, a fact that, repeated in less-extreme form at elite colleges around the country, has led to widespread calls to supplement or even replace race-based affirmative action with class-based affirmative action.

Unfortunately, class-based affirmative action has its own problems. For one thing, the whole idea of affirmative action is based on proportionate representation and if poor and middle-class people were proportionately represented in elite colleges, the first thing that would happen is that most of the current students would need to leave. At Harvard today only 17 percent come from the bottom 60 percent of the population; at a Harvard that had achieved not only racial but economic diversity, 60 percent of the students would come from the bottom 60 percent of the population. That leaves out a lot of outraged rich people. And the second thing that would happen is that most of the colleges would go broke. The newly enrolled bottom 60 percent would consist entirely of people from households making less than $65,000 a year (which is almost exactly what a year's tuition and room and board costs) and while it's no doubt true that a few superrich schools like Harvard could afford to subsidize their newly impoverished student body, the vast majority of the merely wealthy ones would sink like stones.

So when people talk about class-based affirmative action, what they're really talking about is adding a few more poor kids to the mix. Which is why people who really care about everyone having a chance to succeed are increasingly committed to making at least some or maybe even all public higher education free to everyone. As President Obama puts it: "Earning a post-secondary degree or credential is no longer just a pathway to opportunity for a talented few; rather, it is a prerequisite for the growing jobs of the new economy. Over this decade, employment in jobs requiring education beyond a high school diploma will grow more rapidly than employment in jobs that do not; of the thirty fastest-growing occupations, more than half require postsecondary education. With the average earnings of college graduates at a level that is twice as high as that of workers with only a high school diploma, higher education is now the clearest pathway into the middle class."

From this standpoint, the unfairness of the current system is pretty obvious. The students coming into college are from economically advantaged families; the students coming out of college perpetuate that advantage. So the way to make the system fairer is to make it possible for everyone to go to college, giving everyone a chance at those rapidly growing jobs that require a postsecondary education.

But the problem with this scenario is even more fundamental than the problem with economic diversity, and, although President Obama appears not to recognize it, it's a problem with the jobs, not the universities. On the Bureau of Labor Statistics's list of the fastest-growing occupations, number one is industrial-organizational psychologists. Even after reading their job description—"Apply principles of psychology to human resources, management, sales and marketing problems . . . work with management to . . . improve worker productivity"—I admit I'm still not totally sure what they do. But they get paid well for doing it: their median salary is $83,580 a year, well worth the required four years of college and several years of postgraduate work. The only downside is that there are only about 1,100 industrial-organizational psychologists right now and even at the rate demand is growing, ten years from now, only 2,000 will be needed.[9]

So let's go the second-fastest-growing job, personal care aides. The good news here is that there are a lot of these jobs and there will be a lot more: almost 1.2 million now, almost 1.8 million by 2022. The bad news is these jobs don't require a college degree (or even a high school degree), and the pay sucks. The median salary is $19,910 a year, and it isn't getting better. In fact, it's getting worse. A recent report says that since

2009, low-wage jobs have been becoming even-lower-wage jobs and that "wage declines" have been especially pronounced for janitors and cleaners, personal care aides, home health aides and maids and housekeeping cleaners.[10] All these jobs are growing; they don't pay well and they don't require a college degree. Indeed, in 2012, only a little over 20 percent of jobs required a Bachelor of Arts degree: in 2022, that number will be virtually unchanged.

So the reason to get a college degree is not to prepare for the jobs of the future; most of them won't require one. It's to have a shot at the *good* jobs of the future, and it's no doubt true that making a four-year college education available to everyone who wanted one would probably give more people a real shot at those good jobs. Right now, the people who end up as personal and home care aides are predominantly women of color from poor families. They never had the chance to go to college to better themselves. But if college were free, they would have that chance, and some of them would be doctors and lawyers and nurses and organizational psychologists. Some of them would even be CEOs. The health care industry pays its CEOs very well—their median income is $13.6 million a year. Right now, there probably isn't even one black woman in the health care industry making that kind of money. If everyone had an equal opportunity to qualify themselves for those jobs, there'd be a bunch of them, around 6.5 percent of the total.

But of course, the vast majority of people working in health care—black women, white women, white men, Latinos and Latinas—would not be earning $13.6 million a year. They'd be earning $9.38 an hour. Making equality of opportunity real would diversify both the bosses and the workers but it wouldn't reduce the gap between them; the workers would still be paid so badly that more than half of them would have to rely on some sort of public assistance to make ends meet. And the high pay of the bosses would be directly related to the low pay of the workers. One of the central challenges facing health care employers today, says an expert on the industry, is "finding people to work for you at a wage where you can be profitable."[11] In other words, the reason your boss gets paid so much is as a reward for getting you to work so cheap. It's because you only make one six-hundredth of what she does that she has met her challenge.

The word for this challenge is not discrimination, it's exploitation: the fact that the work you're doing is worth more than what you're being paid to do it. And you can't solve the problem of exploitation by giving everyone a fair chance to become an exploiter.

Thus the trouble with education and the trouble with diversity are the same trouble. The White House says a good education is the "pathway to the middle class," and it wants to make that path wider. But with an economy that produces many more low-wage jobs than high-wage ones (48 percent of the new jobs generated in 2013—the year for which we have the most recent figures—paid $15 an hour or less) making the path wider doesn't produce more rich people, it just produces better-educated poor people. A bartender with a Ph.D., as John Marsh has observed, gets paid bartender wages, not the wages of a professor. And these days, many of the Ph.D. holders who *are* professors are also making bartender wages. If the college class you're reading this book in is a class for first-year students, your professor may well be a Ph.D. working on a one-year contract and making less than $35,000 a year. She not only went to college, she was a really good student—ask her how well that's working out.

Education is essentially a sorting system. It's a very unfair sorting system (since it mainly functions to make sure that the wealthy children of wealthy parents stay wealthy), but even if we managed to make it perfectly fair, it would still do nothing but put a small minority on the road to good jobs and a big majority on the road to bad ones. Similarly, the only thing diversity does is try to make sure that the ones who do get the good jobs aren't all white men and the ones who get the bad jobs aren't mainly women of color, which it isn't very successful at doing. But even a successful commitment to diversity would (like everyone going to college) be of absolutely no use to everybody of all races and genders who ended up serving fast food, taking care of old people, selling clothes to young people in malls, etc.

What the commitment to education and the commitment to diversity have in common, in other words, is that their goal is not to minimize inequality but to legitimate it, not to make sure that no one is stuck in poverty but to make sure that no one is stuck in poverty because of their race or their gender or the fact that they couldn't go to college.

So if education and diversity are just different ways of trying to make inequality seem fair, what are some ways of trying instead to diminish it? What should we do if we're more committed to eliminating poverty than to figuring out who deserves to be poor? Maybe, instead of emphasizing ways to avoid the bad jobs ("go to college!") we should start thinking about ways to make the bad jobs better. This graph shows the relation between the productivity of American workers (basically the amount of income their labor generates) and their pay. From 1948 until 1973, productivity and pay were growing in sync; since then, productivity has continued to rise while pay has flatlined.

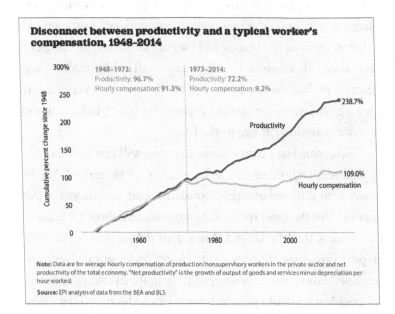

Disconnect between productivity and a typical worker's compensation, 1948–2014

1948–1973:
Productivity: 96.7%
Hourly compensation: 91.3%

1973–2014:
Productivity: 72.2%
Hourly compensation: 9.2%

Productivity — 238.7%

Hourly compensation — 109.0%

Cumulative percent change since 1948

Note: Data are for average hourly compensation of production/nonsupervisory workers in the private sector and net productivity of the total economy. "Net productivity" is the growth of output of goods and services minus depreciation per hour worked.

Source: EPI analysis of data from the BEA and BLS

Where has the income generated by those workers gone? It hasn't disappeared; it's just been redistributed. Instead of going to typical workers, it has gone either to bosses or to owners. That's what rising inequality is: the increasing gap between what the work is worth and what, on the one hand, the many workers get and, on the other hand, the few bosses and owners get.

If, during this period, you've been worried about the glass

ceiling, about the forms of discrimination that make it difficult for women or minorities to become bosses and owners of capital, you haven't been concerned about economic inequality at all. Not to put too fine a point on it, what you've actually been worrying about is the fact that not enough women and people of color have been afforded the opportunity to extract profits from (i.e., rip off) the vast majority of workers. And while it's easy to see how the bosses and owners might start feeling better about themselves if they weren't all white males ("see, everybody has the chance to rise to the top!"), it's very hard to see why this should matter to anyone else (since, in fact, almost no one actually will rise to the top).

Now, this last claim—almost no one will rise to the top—might seem a little unfair, at least to the 64 percent of Americans who still believe that upward social mobility is a live option. But the most recent data suggests that those 64 percent are wrong, that the United States is, as the authors of the 2015 report *Economic Mobility in the United States* put it, "very immobile." And even if there were more mobility, the percentage of people who could benefit from it would be tiny. That's why health-care workers, fast-food workers, sales people, shuttle drivers for Facebook, Apple and eBay, writers for Web sites like *Gawker* and *Salon* and adjunct faculty for universities like Tufts, Georgetown, the University of Oregon or (where I work) the University of Illinois at Chicago, do not need the false promise that they can somehow get different and better jobs. These are the jobs they have, and these are the jobs that exist. What we need is to make these jobs better.

So take a look at this second graph.

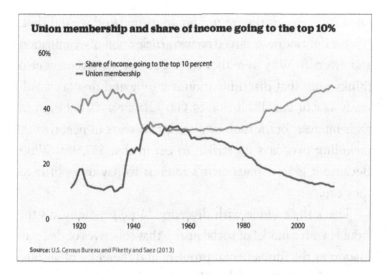

What it shows is the inverse relation between the share of income going to the top not 1 but 10 percent and membership in labor unions. And what it suggests is one strategy for workers to reclaim the fruits of their productivity, to get back the income they've earned: organize. Presumably no one thinks unions are a panacea, but it's hard not to be impressed by the fact that, according to the Bureau of Labor Statistics, the weekly median salary of union members (in 2014) was $970 and the weekly salary of non-union members was $763.[12] When we organized a union at the University of Illinois at Chicago, the salary earned by most of the lecturers who taught first-year writing was $30,000; after we signed our first contract, it was $37,500.

And the experience of getting that contract was an educational one. A standard bargaining strategy is for the two parties to try early on to reach agreement on some of the easy issues, issues they're not far apart on. And we did that. Almost right away we agreed on two articles: non-discrimination and diversity. Why were they easy? Because management also thinks both that discrimination is wrong and that (as we already saw in our discussion of Gary Becker) it's not even in their interest. But it took us almost two years of negotiating, including two days on strike, to get to that $37,500. Why? Because it is in management's interest to pay us as little as they can.

That's the trouble with diversity. More generally, it's the trouble with a model of social justice that conceives of discrimination as the fundamental problem and therefore of antidiscrimination as the solution. That model of justice is a deeply conservative one, geared not to eliminating or even minimizing poverty but just to reallocating it. Furthermore it isn't even good at that. Black people today are economically worse off than they were ten years ago but not because there's been an increase in racism. It's because the last ten years have been hardest on poor people and black people were already disproportionately poor. Thus a serious and entirely race-blind transfer of wealth to poor people (even just the $15 dollar an hour minimum wage and even though the majority of people working for minimum wage are white) would do more to benefit poor black people than would the most rigorous and effective enactment and enforcement of every possible antidiscrimination law.

The New York Times has called 2015 "the year we obsessed over identity." And it's true that a year in which Bruce Jenner turned into Caitlyn Jenner while Rachel Dolezal, a woman who'd always presented as black, was outed as white, has offered many opportunities to indulge that obsession. Certainly a lot could be said about why so many people celebrated Jenner declaring she was transgender while almost no one was prepared to accept Dolezal as transracial. But the truth is that almost every year in America—and increasingly every year in every country whose economy looks like ours—is a year in which we obsess over identity. In part, this is a good thing. If obsessing about what gender people identify as can get us to stop punishing them for identifications some of us may disapprove of, that's a step in the right direction. But insofar as—in a world where the gap between the rich and the poor keeps on getting worse—the obsession with identity distracts us from that gap or, worse still, tells us a false but comforting story about it, identity becomes part of the problem not the solution. What we like to think is that racism (or anyway, racism plus sexism, plus homophobia, etc.) is primarily responsible for American inequality. And the reason we like it (the reason it's comforting) is because we can all disapprove of racism, and even if it's proving very difficult to actually get rid of it, we can all—rich and poor—agree that it would be a good thing if we did. Just look around your classroom, or your office, or your living room—see if anyone raises their hand to defend white supremacy.

But racism doesn't create the world in which the people who actually take care of your sick grandmother make so much less than the people who run and own the company they work for. Capitalism does. Sexism hasn't created the (small) class of people who can send their children to elite colleges. Capitalism has. Homophobia didn't make the inflation-adjusted median income of American households decline by $3,000 dollars from the time I started writing this book till now. Capitalism did. And, unlike white supremacy, capitalism has its defenders. Any serious conversation about how to make the U.S. a more equal society has to start by talking about the real causes of our inequality. The biggest trouble with diversity is that it keeps us from talking about the trouble with capitalism.

Acknowledgments

Although this book derives in part from the academic work I've been doing for some time, I would never have written it if I hadn't moved to the University of Illinois at Chicago five years ago. Not only my colleagues and students in the English Department but people from around the university (especially the members of the 2010 committee) have made a fundamental contribution. And the effort of UIC as an institution to confront a daunting but exciting set of challenges has been a continuous inspiration.

More individuated thanks are due the faculty with whom I've team-taught seminars: Ralph Cintron, Lennard Davis, and Deirdre McCloskey from UIC, and Kenneth Warren from the University of Chicago. I'm grateful also to the students who took those seminars (especially Scott MacFarland, who came through with some invaluable last-minute research assistance), and to both the audiences at the many universities where parts of the book were first presented as lectures and the publications (the *New York Times, ALH* and *n+1*) where portions of chapters 2 and 3 first appeared in different form.

Many other friends, colleagues and students made contributions in less formal contexts. Several dinners were enlivened (a term I prefer to the more usual formulation, "wrecked") by discussion of the issues raised in this book. Special thanks here go to Jane Weinstock, Jim Welling, Liz Davis, Steve Weinstein, Ruth Leys, Michael Fried, Joseph Bartscherer, Diane Shamash, Oren Izenberg, Sonya Rasminski, Jan and Pam Michaels, Roz and Michael Lieb, Cathy Birkenstein-Graff, Jerry Graff, Mary Beth Rose, Leon Fink, Sue Levine, Ellen and Michael Tanner, Jane Tompkins, Stanley Fish and Jennifer Ashton. Others were influential in even less formal settings; thanks here to Anna Brown, Nicholas Brown, Madhu Dubey, Mark Friedman, Jack Kerkering, Mary Lindsey, Becky Michaels, Jonathan Michaels, Peter Michaels, Sascha Michaels, Tom Moss, Yasmin Nair, Ben Nugent, Jason Potts, Adolph Reed, Bridget Tsemo and Vershawn Young.

Stanley Fish has already appeared on the dinner party list, and he should also have appeared on the co-teaching one; indeed, where none of my other co-teachers can be blamed for anything in this book, it will be obvious to readers of my chapter on religion and politics that a lot of it can be blamed on Stanley. More important, it was Stanley who brought me to UIC and who then encouraged me, in his usual abusive way, to write for a more general audience. There are a lot of books called *The Trouble with* something but if mine pays tribute to any of the others, it's to *The Trouble with Principle* and, more generally, to Stanley's efforts to make the idea of the public intellectual a little less dispiriting. *The Trouble with Diversity* would never have been written without his model and his presence.

It also wouldn't have been written, or even conceived, without the entrepreneurial energy and critical intelligence of my agent, Melissa Flashman. Thank God she decided not to stay in graduate school. And, finally, *The Trouble with Diversity* would never have been completed without the extraordinary efforts of my editor, Sara Bershtel, whose intelligence is exceeded only by her perseverance. Thanks as well to the uncompromising (but in a nice way) Riva Hocherman and to everyone at Metropolitan, especially Kate Levin.

Notes

INTRODUCTION

1. Consciousness of color was, it goes without saying, always central to American society insofar as that society was a committedly racist one. The relevant change here—marked rather than produced by *Bakke*—involved (in the wake of both the successes and failures of the civil rights movement) the emergence of color consciousness as an antiracist position. The renewed black nationalism in the 1960s is one standard example of this transition, but the phenomenon is more general. You can get a striking sense of it by reading John Okada's *No-No Boy*, a novel about the Japanese Americans who answered no to the two loyalty questions on the questionnaire administered to them at the relocation centers they were sent to during World War II. The novel itself, published in 1957, is a pure product of the civil rights movement, determined to overcome race (and ignore class) in the imagination of a world in which people are utterly individualized—"only people." It began to become important, however, as an expression of what Frank Chin, in an article written in 1976 and included as an appendix to the current

edition, calls "yellow soul," and when it's taught today in Asian American literature classes, reading it counts toward the fulfillment of diversity requirements that Okada himself would not have understood.

2. Simi Linton, *Claiming Disability* (New York: New York University Press, 1998), 96.

3. The relations between race and class have been an important topic in American writing at least since the 1930s, and in recent years they have, in the more general form of the relations between identity and inequality, been the subject of an ongoing academic discussion. Some of the more notable contributions include *Culture and Equality* (2000) by Brian Barry, *Redistribution or Recognition* (2003), an exchange between Nancy Fraser and Axel Honneth, and *The Debate on Classes* (1990), featuring an important essay by Erik Olin Wright and a series of exchanges about that essay. And in my particular field of specialization, American literature, Gavin Jones is about to publish an important and relevant book called *American Hunger*. I cite these texts in particular because, in quite different ways, they share at least some of my skepticism about the value of identity. And I have myself written in an academic context about these issues, most recently in *The Shape of the Signifier* (2004). *The Trouble with Diversity* is in part an effort to make some of the terms of this discussion more vivid to a more general audience. More important, however, it is meant to advance a particular position in that discussion, an argument that the concept of identity is incoherent and that its continuing success is a function of its utility to neoliberalism.

4. *The Economist,* December 29, 2004.

5. David Brooks, *New York Times,* November 10, 2005; Janny Scott and David Leonhardt in *Class Matters* (New York: Times Books, Henry Holt, 2005), 13–14. The articles collected in *Class Matters* were originally published in the *Times* in the spring and summer of 2005. Parallel series ran in the *Wall Street Journal* and the *Los Angeles Times;* the *Washington Post* is running one now (spring 2006). Although, as my discussion in the text makes clear, I'm skeptical about some of this interest, all in all it seems to me a very

good thing. And there are many other people (e.g., Dalton Conley, Barbara Ehrenreich, Thomas Frank, Paul Krugman, Annette Lareau, Kevin Phillips, Adolph Reed and Kenneth Warren, just to mention a few) trying to put the emphasis back where I too believe it belongs.

6. *New York Times,* October 6, 2005.

7. Quoted in *Diversity Inc.,* September 12, 2005.

8. Jonathan Marks, *The Realities of Races,* published in a Web forum called *Is Race "Real"?* organized by the Social Sciences Research Council: http://www.raceandgenomics.ssrc.org/Marks/.

CHAPTER 1. THE TROUBLE WITH RACE

1. My discussion here relies on Charles Lofgren, *The Plessy Case* (New York: Oxford University Press, 1987).

2. The facts in this case are usefully summarized in F. James Davis, *Who Is Black?* (University Park: Pennsylvania State University Press, 1991), 8–11.

3. Quoted in Lothrop Stoddard, *The Rising Tide of Color Against White World-Supremacy* (New York: Scribner's, 1920), 183.

4. *The Race Myth* is the title of a book by the evolutionary biologist Joseph Graves (New York: Penguin, 2004). R. C. Lewontin is Alexander Agassiz Professor Emeritus of Biology at Harvard University and has been influential in criticizing race as a biological term for over thirty years. The citation here is from "Confusions About Human Races," his contribution to the *Is Race "Real"?* Web forum cited in the introduction, note 8. The purpose of the forum was to respond to recent attempts (especially by Armand Leroi, writing in the *New York Times*) to revive race as a biological concept. As of this writing, I think it's fair to say that Lewontin, Graves and some of the other writers cited below are fairly typical of the current scientific skepticism about race.

5. Graves, *The Race Myth,* 17.

6. Adolph Reed, "Making Sense of Race, I: The Ideology of Race, the Biology of Human Variation and the Problem of Medical and Public Health Research," *Journal of Race and Policy* (Spring–Summer

2005, 16). Furthermore, not all the people in the relevant population actually have the trait. So when we think about medical intervention, what we're interested in is less whether a person is likely
to benefit than whether the person actually will benefit, and increased knowledge about genomics makes the racial distinction
even less relevant. "Imagine, for example," Jonathan Marks says (in *Is
Race "Real"?*), "that there is an allele that affects the ability of a drug
to work. How can we expect it to be distributed in the human species? As an African version and a European version? As a Basque or
Ashkenazi version and a wild-type? Of course not—rather, we must
expect it to be distributed in a similar fashion to all the genetic variation we are already familiar with. That is to say, we might expect to
find the allele in 22 percent of Africans and in 54 percent of Europeans. Of what benefit would racialized medicine then possibly
be? The therapeutic intervention would have to be based on the
genotype, not on any racialized identity. Otherwise it would be far
more likely to kill people than to cure them."

7. Jean-Paul Sartre, *Anti-Semite and Jew* (New York: Schocken,
1995), 37, 69. For further discussion of Sartre and, in particular, of
the difference between what it means to belong to a race and what
it means to belong to a class, see Walter Benn Michaels, "Autobiography of an Ex-White Man," *Transition,* issue 73, vol. 7, no. 1 (1998).

8. Adrian Piper, *Out of Order, Out of Sight,* vol. 1, *Selected Writ-
ings in Meta-Art, 1968–1992* (Cambridge: MIT Press, 1996), 305.

9. Southern Reporter, 2nd series, vol. 479, 372, 1985.

10. See *Federal Register Notice,* October 30, 1997, "Revisions to
the Standards for the Classification of Federal Data on Race and Ethnicity" at http://www.whitehouse.gov/omb/fedreg/ombdir15.html.

11. The parents, in other words, were not social constructionists.
They thought of themselves and hence of their daughter (even though
she didn't know it) as passing.

12. The most recent (January 2004) federal "worksheet" for
mothers asks them to identify their own race (more precisely, the
race they "consider" themselves to be) as well as the race they consider the father to be. The mother's race is then used to designate

the child's race. http://www.cdc.gov/nchs/data/dvs/momswkstf
_improv.pdf.

13. In his contribution to David Theo Goldberg's *Anatomy of
Racism,* Kwame Anthony Appiah, whose skepticism about the co-
herence of racial identity has been a longstanding influence on my
writing, reminds us that we used to think that some people were
witches and we treated them as if they were witches, sometimes even
describing them as having witch blood and sometimes even burning them as witches. Later we figured out they weren't witches, and
there wasn't any such thing as witch blood. But this didn't mean that
we had stopped being prejudiced against witches; it meant that we
had stopped believing in witches. And when we discovered that there
wasn't any such thing as witch blood, we didn't decide that witches
were a social reality rather than a biological one. We didn't think that
a witch was someone whom other people considered a witch, and
we don't even think that a witch is someone who considers herself a
witch. What we think is that people who consider themselves witches
are mistaken. And if we don't think that there's any such thing as
white blood, we ought to start thinking that people who consider
themselves white are mistaken too.

14. Richard T. Ford, *Racial Culture* (Princeton, N.J.: Princeton
University Press, 2005), 72.

15. This is why, with respect to race, assimilation is a false issue—
why a black person acting white is not the same as a gay person
acting straight. There is no behavior that goes with being black or
being white, so you can't successfully explain or justify your behavior by alluding to your identity. You can't say, I do this because I'm
black. But there obviously is some behavior that goes with being
gay or straight. And yet it still doesn't work to justify your behavior.
You can't say that you're a man who likes sleeping with women
because you're straight; liking to sleep with women is synonymous
with what it means to be a straight male.

16. Or French, even though, as we've already seen, French
Canadians are also at relatively high risk for Tay-Sachs.

17. The idea of heritage depends on taking some acts and events

from the historical past and claiming them as ours and some other acts and events from the historical past and assigning them to someone else. But, of course, none of these acts was actually performed by us, so the principle of assignment is always up for grabs: why should some things that I didn't do count as part of my history while some other things that I also didn't do count as someone else's history? There are, inevitably, innumerable ways of making these assignments. Sometimes what, say, Queen Elizabeth I did or was is part of my history (she spoke English, I speak English); sometimes it isn't (she was English, I'm American); sometimes it is again (she was a woman, I'm a woman); or it still isn't (I'm a man); or it is again (she was white, I'm white). My point, obviously, is that the choice among these divisions is essentially arbitrary, and that because we can multiply both similarities and differences endlessly (she liked roast beef, I . . .), it makes no real sense to say that the queen does belong to some people's history and doesn't belong to others'. The more general point would be that there is no such thing as our history (as my history and your history); there's only history. But even if the national and sexual and culinary links are arbitrary, at least they're real: there are (by law) such things as British citizens, and there are (in nature) women and people who like roast beef. But there are no longer any laws that tell us which race is ours, and the need for culture and for the idea of cultural heritage is produced in the first place by our skepticism about whether there are such things as races in nature. So it makes more sense to claim the people who liked roast beef for our culture than it does to claim white or black people.

18. Michael Omi and Howard Winant, *Racial Formation in the United States* (New York: Routledge, 1986), 6, 62.

CHAPTER 2. OUR FAVORITE VICTIMS

1. Philip Roth, *The Plot Against America* (Boston: Houghton Mifflin, 2005), 65, 69.

2. Justice Harlan's dissent in *Plessy* makes this point explicitly and indignantly when he complains that the Louisiana law separating blacks and whites allowed the Chinese—"a race so different from

our own that we do not permit those belonging to it to become citizens"—to ride with whites. An important reason for this was no doubt the fact that the Asian population of the United States in 1890 was statistically insignificant—only 109,514 people. The number of blacks, by contrast, was almost 7.5 million. The great explosion of the Asian population in the United States did not take place until after the Immigration Act of 1965, and it is both the terms of this act (which made educational status and the ability to make an economic contribution the central criteria in determining eligibility for immigration) and the historical moment in which it was produced (the height of the civil rights movement) that have helped make the modern Asian American experience in the United States (Asian Americans are the richest group measured in the census) so different from the African American experience.

3. Malcolm X, *The Autobiography of Malcolm X,* as told to Alex Haley (New York: Ballantine Books, 1973), 399. Keith Gessen, the most penetrating of the reviewers to point out that "[m]any of the things Roth imagines happening to the Jews under Lindbergh have in fact happened in this country—to blacks," goes on to cite James Baldwin on the irrelevance of the Holocaust to the black experience in America. (Keith Gessen, "Philip Roth's Jewish Problem: The Plot Against America" http://newyorkmetro.com/nymetro /arts/books/reviews/9902/index2.htm.) But Malcolm X is making a stronger claim than Baldwin's, not just that groups like the Jews are tolerated in American society but that they are turned into white people.

4. Thomas Dixon, *The Leopard's Spots* (New York: Doubleday, Page, 1902), 442.

5. Thomas Dixon, *The Traitor* (New York: Doubleday, Page, 1907), 328. The chapter is called "The Day of Atonement."

6. Khalid Abdul Muhammad, quoted in "Conspiracies in Common," *The Nizkor Project,* http://www.nizkor.org/hweb/orgs.

7. There is, however, a museum called America's Black Holocaust Museum in Milwaukee, Wisconsin, which features such exhibits as the reproduction of the cargo hold of a slave ship and a

tribute to the museum's founder, Dr. James Cameron (who in 1930 escaped a lynching in Indiana; two others were killed).

8. Gode Davis and James Fortier, http://www.americanlynching .com.

9. Other immigrant groups also benefited, but it's not hard to recognize that Jews, who had the most to lose (anti-Semitism in eastern Europe and Germany was the closest thing to American Negrophobia and would turn out to be in certain obvious respects even worse), also had the most to gain. Jews were fleeing prejudice to come to the United States; Italians and Greeks and Japanese and Chinese (not to mention Africans) were not. In this respect, the history of the Jews in America really is a history of their triumph over prejudice, but the prejudice is European and they triumphed over it just by coming here. The African story is just the opposite.

10. Watson is quoted in Albert S. Lindemann, *The Jew Accused* (Cambridge: Cambridge University Press, 1991), 235. Watson goes on to say that the case has also "shown us how differently the law deals with rich man and poor." Lindemann's account of Frank's salary is on p. 239. Lindemann's view of the Frank case is that anti-Semitism "did come into play" but its role was "not decisive" (237).

11. Steve Oney, *And the Dead Shall Rise* (New York: Pantheon Books, 2003), 9. Oney has an extremely useful discussion of the debate about child labor during the period, in the course of which he quotes the then president of Coca-Cola, Asa G. Candler, saying, "The most beautiful sight we see is the child at labor; as early as he may get at labor the more beautiful, the more useful does his life get to be." "In this," Oney concludes, "the National Pencil Company—whose 170-member workforce consisted largely of teenage girls—was perfectly in step" (15–16).

12. Lindemann, *The Jew Accused,* 239.

13. The report, written by Sarah Anderson, John Cavanagh, Scott Klinger and Liz Stanton (and available online at http://www .faireconomy.org), includes the useful observation that if the pay of workers had grown at the same rate as the pay of CEOs, "in 2004, the average worker would have made $110,136, compared to the

actual average of $27,460. Similarly, if the federal minimum wage had grown at the same rate as CEO pay, it would have been $23.03 in 2004, instead of $5.15."

14. http://www.doi.gov/diversity/workforce_diversity.html.

15. http://www.fbi.gov/ucr/ucr.htm#hate.

16. Charles Chesnutt, *The Marrow of Tradition* (New York: Penguin, 1993), 61.

17. *Lochner v. New York,* 198 U.S. 45 (1905).

18. Quoted in Joel Williamson, *The Crucible of Race* (New York: Oxford University Press, 1984), 128.

19. Andrew Macdonald, *The Turner Diaries* (Arlington, Va.: National Vanguard Books, 1978), 161. Andrew Macdonald was the pen name for the white racist leader William L. Pierce.

20. Andrew Macdonald, *Hunter* (Hillsboro, W.Va.: National Vanguard Books, 1989), 99. It's worth pointing out that Pierce's hostility to Jews was completely compatible with hostility to Christianity, which he blames on the Jews and which he calls "a religion of equality, of weakness . . . of surrender and submission, of oblivion. If our race survives the next century," says one of the characters in *Hunter,* "it will be because we have gotten the monkey of Christianity off our backs" (105).

21. Daniel Pipes, "The New Anti-Semitism." This article was originally published in the *Jewish Exponent,* October 16, 1997, and is available on Pipes's Web site, http://www.danielpipes.org/article/288.

22. http://abcnews.go.com/Nightline/Nightline25/story?id=273599.

23. Kenneth Warren, *So Black and Blue: Ralph Ellison and the Occasion of Criticism* (Chicago: University of Chicago Press, 2003), 77.

24. Think Cornel West, having parked his "rather elegant" car in a "safe" lot in midtown Manhattan and wearing a very beautiful three-piece black suit, trying to get a cab to 115th Street, where he's supposed to get his picture taken for the cover of his new book. He is naturally and justifiably infuriated by the fact that ten empty and available cabs pass him by. His problem, as the sociologist Annette Lareau brilliantly puts it, is his "inability to signal" his

"class position" (*Unequal Childhoods: Class, Race and Family Life* [Berkeley: University of California Press, 2003] 240). In situations like this one, Lareau says, "race trumps social class." The obvious irony is that West wants his class to matter on the way to a photo shoot for a book that will be called *Race Matters*. The real problem, however, is that a world where rich black people could signal their class as well as rich white people can wouldn't exactly (from the standpoint of equality) be a better world. It's also worth saying here that although West's persistent commitment to advancing a progressive politics through "revitalizing our public conversation about race" (*Race Matters* [New York: Vintage, 2001], 158) seems to me exactly wrong and thus makes him an occasional target of my argument, I respect both the persistence and the ultimate goal.

25. *Adarand Constructors v. Pena* (93-1841), 515 U.S. 200 (1995). The significance of the case was in its holding that "all racial classifications, imposed by whatever federal, state, or local government actor, must be analyzed by a reviewing court under strict scrutiny." Justice Sandra Day O'Connor wrote the majority opinion; Justice Antonin Scalia's remarks are from his concurring opinion.

26. Half the income earned in America in 2004 was earned by the top 20 percent of households; 3.4 percent of it was earned by the bottom 20 percent. (In 1979, the equivalent figures were 43.8 percent and 4 percent.) But that's the comparatively good news. In 2004, the top quintile controlled a little under 85 percent of all the wealth in the country; the whole rest of the country (that is, the other 80 percent of the population) controlled the remaining 15 percent. Or actually, most of the rest of the country did; the bottom quintile didn't—they controlled 0 percent.

27. David Brooks, *New York Times,* October 20, 2005.

28. Robin Givhan, *Washington Post,* June 24, 2005.

CHAPTER 3. RICHER, NOT BETTER

1. The more commonly used figure, median household income per year, is $44,839. http://www.census.gov/Press-release/www/releases/archives/income_wealth/005647.html.

2. Harvard is also, according to the *Harvard Crimson* (April 18, 2006), developing plans to address the needs of what the dean of admissions calls the "middle-income group," "students whose families earn between $110,000 and $200,000 a year."

3. Peter Hong, *Los Angeles Times,* March 19, 2006.

4. Actually, it's "now over $30,000," the founder of IvyWise, Katherine Cohen, told the *New York Times* reporter Dinitia Smith (*New York Times,* April 6, 2006). As I write this, just after the college admissions season for 2006 has ended, people are throwing public fits about the difficulty of getting into the elite colleges (applications are up) and the difficulty of paying for them (tuitions are up) even though the first complaint, obviously, takes some of the wind out of the second's sails—people are lining up to pay the supposedly outrageous prices.

5. Dave Newbart, *Chicago Sun-Times,* June 13, 2004.

6. Donald E. Heller and Christopher J. Rasmussen, "Merit Scholarships and College Access: Evidence from Florida and Michigan," in *Who Should We Help? The Negative Social Consequences of Merit Aid Scholarships,* ed. Donald E. Heller and Patricia Martin, http://www.civilrightsproject.harvard.edu/research/meritaid/fullreport.php. This collection emerged from a conference held at Harvard in 2001 and was made available online in 2002. The Heller and Rasmussen contribution cited in the text makes up chapter 2.

7. The trend toward merit scholarships has been matched by a move away from race-based scholarships, and while it is no doubt obvious by now that I'm opposed to race-based scholarships, it should also be obvious that my opposition to them and to affirmative action more generally has nothing whatever to do with the complaint that it's a form of discrimination against whites. When, for example, the president of the NAACP Legal Defense and Educational Fund responds to recent efforts to open scholarship programs for black students to white students as well, I think he is absolutely right to wonder how anyone can possibly "conclude that the great evil in this country is discrimination against white people" (*New York Times,* March 14, 2006). Where he's wrong, however, is in thinking that the

great evil is discrimination against black students instead. Or, more precisely, where he's wrong is in thinking that the problem is one of discrimination. It's poor kids, not black kids, who are being penalized, and they're the victims of bad educations, not discrimination. Ideally, all scholarships would be need-based, and the transfer of scholarship money from people who need it to people who don't would be ended. In the meantime, however (and on the principle of need), race-based scholarships are preferable to merit scholarships, since if you used race in awarding the money, more poor kids would get it. Grosse Ile, for example, is 99 percent white, whereas Hamtramck is only 61 percent white.

8. *Chicago Tribune,* November 18, 2003.

9. *New York Times,* February 7, 2004.

10. As reported on http://www.thelawyer.com/cgi-bin/item.cgi ?id=119184&d=122&h=24&f=46.

11. Curtis Sittenfeld, *Prep* (New York: Random House, 2005), 16.

12. Tom Wolfe, *I Am Charlotte Simmons* (New York: Farrar, Straus and Giroux, 2004), 75.

13. Lionel Trilling, *The Liberal Imagination* (New York: Doubleday Anchor, 1950), 212.

14. *Prep,* 362.

15. *Harvard Crimson,* March 10, 2005.

16. Richard D. Kahlenberg, *Left Behind: Unequal Opportunity in Higher Education,* 9. This is from the Century Foundation Web site: http://www.tcf.org.

17. Trilling's "Manners, Morals, and the Novel," the essay in *The Liberal Imagination* that addresses this question of class, was first written for a conference at Kenyon College in 1947.

18. It's sometimes argued that going to elite schools isn't as important as we think because it can be shown that students who were admitted to elite schools but chose (for whatever reason) to go to less elite ones do just as well as the students who actually attend the elite schools. This may be bad news for the elite colleges, but it doesn't affect my point; it just shows that the benefits of inequality have been conferred before college even begins. That's why the real victims are

not those who are too poor to pay the tuition at elite schools once they're admitted (a dying breed, in any event) but those who are too poor to pay for the advantages (the private schools, the travel soccer teams, the SAT coaches, etc.) that might get them admitted in the first place (and that will make them successful even if they end up going to less elite colleges).

19. Nicholas Lemann, *The Big Test* (New York: Farrar, Straus and Giroux, 2000), 271.

20. Dalton Conley, *Being Black, Living in the Red* (Berkeley: University of California Press, 1999), 7. Another book that comes at the same problem but from a different angle is Annette Lareau's *Unequal Childhoods* (Berkeley: University of California Press, 2003), which, in the course of trying to show the difference class makes in the way we raise our children, also ends up showing the difference race *doesn't* make. Race "mattered less in children's daily lives than did their social class," Lareau writes. "As a middle-class Black boy, Alexander Williams had much more in common with *white* middle-class Garrett Tallinger than he did in common with less-privileged Black boys" (241). Lareau goes on to note that Americans "tend to resist the notion that they live in a society of social classes" but that, "when asked about social divisions," they "readily discuss the power of race" (257). *The Trouble with Diversity* is about the connection between these two facts, about the reasons for and the consequences of our preference for talking about race instead of class.

21. Richard Sennett, *Respect in a World of Inequality* (New York: Norton, 2003), 53.

22. David Brooks, "One Nation, Slightly Divisible," *The Atlantic,* December 2001.

23. The "Campus Culture Initiative," produced in the wake of the alleged rape of a poor, black female student at North Carolina Central College working as a stripper at a party organized by rich white male lacrosse players at Duke, is a textbook case. President Richard Brodhead's eloquent letter to the Duke community articulates his concern not only about racism and sexism at Duke but also "about the deep structures of inequality in our society—inequalities of

wealth, privilege, and opportunity (including educational opportunity), and the attitudes of superiority those inequalities breed" (www .dukenews.edu). His goal, obviously and rightly, is to get Duke students to behave better. But the privilege they enjoy—the inequality from which they benefit—will be in no way diminished by whatever success he may have in getting them to lose what he calls their attitude.

24. And, of course, no right-wing Republican who *had* heard of the word *classism* would dream of saying it in public, since using it would make you sound as if you yourself belonged to the liberal elite.

25. As Rita Felski elegantly puts it, class is "essentially, rather than contingently, a hierarchical concept." Nancy Fraser and John Guillory are among the other writers who have insisted, correctly in my view, on the essential difference between class and culture.

CHAPTER 4. JUST AND UNJUST REWARDS

1. http://www.uslaw.com/library/article/ABAWomenJustice.html.

2. *Chicago Tribune,* June 6, 2005.

3. The full text of the complaint can be found at http://www .newsday.com/business/ny-morgan-suit,0,2997405.acrobat?coll=ny -business-headlines.

4. *Forbes,* July 13, 2004.

5. *New York Times,* July 17, 2004.

6. The precise figure Wal-Mart gives is $9.68, and this number is sometimes contested by people who think it's really lower. For the purposes of the following discussion, however, it's low enough. And it's worth noting that the online publication politicalaffairs.net puts the hourly salary of the CEO (H. Lee Scott Jr.) at $8,434.49. It also provides a useful summary of the hourly pay for some Wal-Mart subcontractors: the low is $0.17 in Bangladesh and China; the high is $0.53 in Swaziland.

7. The Drogin report, *Statistical Analysis of Gender Patterns in Wal-Mart Workforce,* was released in 2003.

8. Amy Farmer, Jill Tiefenthaler and Amandine Sambira, "The Availability and Distribution of Services for Victims of Domestic

Violence in the U.S.," at waltoncollege.uark.edu/lab/AFarmer /services%20RR%20Feb%202004.doc.

9. Kerby Anderson, "Abuse and Domestic Violence" at http:// www.marriagemissions.com/troubled/abuse_domestic_violence .php.

10. Peter T. Kilborn, "The Five-Bedroom, Six-Figure Rootless Life," in *Class Matters* (New York: Henry Holt, 2005), 148.

11. This makes the question of whether people are voting Republican because of "values" (two hours a week of Bible study) or economic interest (two thirds of the residents of Alpharetta earn more than $100,000 a year) an easy one. As long as the two go hand in hand, it doesn't even need to be decided.

12. Other downsides to economic segregation are a little more concrete. School districts in southern Westchester County, according to the *New York Times,* have had to close schools "after just a dusting of snow because more and more of their teachers live in communities 40 or 50 miles to the north, where the housing is cheaper and the snow falls thicker" (April 9, 2006). The same story goes on to talk about the difficulty of staffing volunteer fire departments in towns like Bedford since volunteer firefighters tend to be blue-collar workers and blue-collar workers can't afford to live there. The solution? The townsfolk (doctors, lawyers, stock brokers, investment bankers et al.) have gathered together to refurbish an old "tattered shingle-sided ranch house," which, because it's old, doesn't have to meet the zoning requirements for new housing (a four-acre lot) and can be used to recruit a blue-collar type if he'll volunteer as a fireman.

13. The text of the original press release and of related documents is available at http://www.wachovia.com. Just search for "slavery."

14. *Wall Street Journal,* May 10, 2005.

15. *Chicago Sun-Times,* September 13, 2005. And the skepticism was not alleviated when Lehman Bros. went back, looked harder and found a couple more.

16. The report is available on the Web site. Wachovia is a little

less forthcoming, however, about the present. A watchdog group called the Inner City Press/Community on the Move (ICP) has been unable to obtain either from Wachovia or from the Federal Reserve Board a list of the subprime lenders that Wachovia finances or invests in. The reason it wants the list is that subprime lenders are sometimes involved in predatory lending practices that victimize the poor and (with respect to finance) the ignorant, getting them to pay inflated loan costs. Wachovia argues that making this information public would cause it competitive harm, and the courts have thus far upheld the Federal Reserve Board's decision not to release the names of Wachovia's commercial clients.

Of course, unless you resort to outright trickery, getting people to pay artificially inflated fees is not in itself against federal law. It's only illegal (as anybody who's been reading this chapter will be unsurprised to learn) if you get people who belong to "protected classes" (e.g., African Americans, Hispanics) to pay more than you would charge whites. The crime, in other words, is not so much the predatory practice as it is the unequal application of it; if you prey on white people as well as black ones, you're off the legal hook. Some states, like Connecticut, are trying to enforce laws that are stricter than the federal ones. But the lenders, led by Wachovia, are arguing that federal law supersedes state authority to regulate nationally chartered banks, and so far they're winning. In *Wachovia Bank, N.A. and Wachovia Mortgage Corporation v. John P. Burke, Banking Commissioner of the State of Connecticut,* the U.S. Court of Appeals for the Second Circuit upheld a lower-court ruling that Wachovia did not have to follow Connecticut's antipredatory lending laws.

17. http://www.historyfactory.com.

18. See the *Wall Street Transcript* interview with Weindruch at http://www.history.com.

19. *Jewish World Review,* July 17, 2000.

20. Burt Neuborne, *The Nation,* October 23, 2000.

21. Randall Robinson, *The Debt* (New York: Plume, 2001), 9.

22. And the idea that this is the gap we should be concerned with transcends the reparations movement. The authors of a report

called *Stalling the Dream: Cars, Race and Hurricane Evacuation* concluded that the reason so many black people were left behind by Katrina was that black people were less likely to own cars than white people, and they plausibly linked this to the economic disparity between whites and blacks. As one of the coauthors of the study, Betsy Leondar-Wright, put it, "Only when we have policies that allow . . . people of color who have been left out to build assets, only then are we going to narrow the racial wealth divide" (*Diversity Inc.,* January 12, 2006). It's not the wealth divide that Leondar-Wright sees as the problem; it's the fact that it's racial.

23. Robert Nozick, *Anarchy, State, and Utopia* (New York: Basic Books, 1974), 231. As the title suggests, Nozick was deeply committed to the smallest possible state; in fact, his idea of utopia was also his idea of what he called the "minimal state." But even he thought that "a more extensive state" (although "socialism," he remarked, "would be going too far") might be necessary ("in the short run") to "rectify" "past injustice." The degree to which addressing the problem of inherited inequality as such requires greater state intervention continues to be controversial. For example, the excellent idea of what gets called a "basic income guarantee" (a minimum income provided to all citizens) is sometimes thought of as increasing state intervention (since the state supplies the money) and sometimes thought of as decreasing it (since the cash makes people responsible for their choices in ways that other forms of welfare, say food stamps, do not).

24. The *New York Times*/CBS Poll reported that 76 percent opposed the tax when no mention was made of the amount of the estates that would be taxed, but that 23 percent supported taxes on estates over $1 million and another 20 percent signed on for estates over $3.5 million (*Class Matters*, 246).

25. Everett Carll Ladd and Karlyn H. Bowman, *Attitudes Toward Economic Opportunity* (Washington, D.C.: AEI Press, 1998), 79.

26. Thomas Frank, *What's the Matter with Kansas?* (New York: Metropolitan Books, 2004), 6.

CHAPTER 5. WHO ARE WE? WHY SHOULD WE CARE?

1. http://www.telegraph.co.uk/news/main.jhtml?xml=/news/2006/01/23/wboliv23.xml.

2. Rutgers Boelens and Hugo de Vos, "Mapuche: Water Law and Indigenous Rights in the Andes." The article originally appeared in *Cultural Survival Quarterly,* vol. 29, no. 4. and is now available online at http://www.unpo.org/news_detail.php?arg=37&par=4073. Private ownership of water rights was a reform introduced in the 1980s and has been resisted both by the indigenous populations, who think of it as a violation of their customs, and by socialists, who don't exactly have customs, but think of it as unjust.

3. Isabel Maria Madaleno, "Aymara Indians in Chile: Water Use in Ancestral Cultures at Odds with Water Rights in Modern Times." This paper was delivered at the Conference on International Agricultural Research in Berlin in October 2004 and is available online at http://www.tropentag.de/2004/abstracts/full/33.pdf.

4. Samuel Huntington, *Who Are We?* (New York: Simon and Schuster, 2004), 13.

5. William L. Pierce, "Enemies on the Right," *National Vanguard Magazine,* no. 116 (August–September 1996). Available online at http://www.natall.com/national-vanguard/116/birch.html.

6. Pierce's organization was the neo-Nazi National Alliance, and the ADL was in a certain sense overstating the case. The alliance itself was mainly a publishing operation, but the books and pamphlets it produced had their effect, not just the Oklahoma City bombing but also the creation of a murderous group called the Order (they killed the talk-show host Alan Berg) and another group called the Aryan Republican Army.

7. Pierce, *The Turner Diaries,* 155, 198.

8. Leslie Marmon Silko, *Almanac of the Dead* (New York: Penguin, 1991), 516.

9. Samuel Huntington, "The Clash of Civilizations?" in *The New Shape of World Politics,* with an introduction by Fareed Zakaria (New York: Norton, 1997), 71.

10. Arthur Schlesinger Jr., *The Disuniting of America* (New York: Norton, 1992), 137.

11. Huntington, *Who Are We?* 365. Huntington's argument is anticipated (in a less alarmist vein; the fear of Mexican immigration had not reached its current proportions) by Michael Lind when, in *The Next American Nation* (New York: Free Press, 1995), he argues against both the multiculturalist and what he calls the "liberal universalist" (5) vision of America. The multiculturalist vision is bad because it fragments American identity and the liberal universalist vision is bad because it ignores American identity altogether, appealing instead to principles like liberty, justice and equality. What Lind wants is what he calls "liberal nationalism" (9) (which he calls loyalty to the "cultural nation"), where the differences between races and the differences between ideologies are subordinated to the differences between nations. So just like Huntington, Lind thinks the relevant choices are between identities, not ideas.

12. Ward Churchill, *Since Predator Came* (Oakland: AK Press, 2005), 326.

13. Ronald Niezen, *The Origins of Indigenism: Human Rights and the Politics of Identity* (Berkeley: University of California Press, 2003), 3.

14. The latest version of this document is available online at http://www.cwis.org/drft9329.html. The passage I cite is from article 8. The *Declaration* begins by affirming "the right of all peoples to be different, to consider themselves different, and to be respected as such."

15. Huntington, *Who Are We?* 159. The remark about language is a quote from Miguel de Unamuno, and the chapter in which this discussion takes place is called "Deconstructing America: The Rise of Subnational Identities." His unhappiness is about the "subnational," not about the "identities."

16. Daniel Nettle and Suzanne Romaine, *Vanishing Voices: The Extinction of the World's Languages* (New York: Oxford University Press, 2000), 7.

17. Mark Abley, *Spoken Here* (Toronto: Vintage Canada, 2003), 4.

18. The identification of language with culture is standard, for several reasons. One is that language really is cultural as opposed to biological (it's the blood of the spirit, not the body). A second is that, unlike, say, cuisine, it's not easily transferable and so trivializable; Chinese can be anyone's favorite food but not just anyone's language. And, lastly (as the discussion that follows will emphasize), languages really are equal. It might make sense to claim, say, that French is the greatest literature, but it cannot really make sense (the views of many French people to the contrary notwithstanding) to claim that French is the greatest language.

19. John Edwards, *Multilingualism* (London: Penguin, 1995), 90, 92.

20. It can't be the case, in other words, that because we speak English, English can count as our descendants' real language. The only way that could possibly be true would be if there were, after all, a kind of genetic propensity that suited certain people to speak certain languages. And although we already noted that no one now believes this (or, anyway, admits to believing it), it's true that people have sometimes acted as if there were such a propensity. The hero of an influential Quebecois nationalist novel of the 1920s (*L'appel de la race* [Montreal: Editions Fides, 1980]) is a Quebecois lawyer who abandoned his roots, married into an English family and gave his children an "Anglo-Saxon" education. When he starts having second thoughts, he begins the process of deanglicizing himself by "relearning his mother tongue" (16). But it's the education of his daughter that makes the real point. For even though she has been brought up speaking English and is, as a teenager, learning French for the first time, it takes her only a few weeks to become fluent in it. French "returns to her," she says, like a language that she had "already known"; "to learn everything," "she has only to look inside her" (41). So the French gene makes French her native language. And if we English speakers are passing on the English gene to our descendants but they end up living in a world where they're all speaking Spanish, they too will have been deprived of their ancestral language.

But, of course, there is no French gene and no English gene

either. Our pretty blue eyes may be an inheritance from our great-great-grandmother, but our language is learned, not inherited. And if all our great-grandchildren end up speaking Spanish instead of English—if everyone in the whole world ends up speaking Spanish and all the other languages of the world die out—no one will have been deprived of his or her heritage; no one will be the victim of any injustice.

21. Charles Taylor, *Multiculturalism and the Politics of Recognition* (Princeton, N.J.: Princeton University Press, 1992), 40.

22. The point here is that the argument for cultural survival can have nothing to do with the quality of the culture (how great its art and literature is) because if it did, we would only want the great cultures to survive. And we wouldn't want them to survive because every culture had a right to survive; we would want them to survive because they were great. Even here, however, it's hard to see why cultural survival is the relevant factor. There are no native speakers of Latin anymore, and people still read Virgil. For that matter, there are no native speakers of the language Shakespeare wrote in anymore, and people still read him, although, increasingly, in translation. The "No Fear Shakespeare" series ("created by Harvard students for students everywhere") gives you the "original text" of the play on the left page, a "line-by-line translation" into English on the right. Many students find these editions, as "Katie, a freshman in college!" says in a customer review, "totally helpful."

23. http://www.cooperativecoffees.com/about/news/clamor20 .html.

24. The occasion for these remarks was an interview between Binh and Christopher Runckel, the first diplomat permanently assigned to Vietnam after the war and now "the principal and founder of Runckel and Associates, a Portland, Oregon-based consulting company that assists businesses to expand their business opportunities in Asia" (http://www.business-in-asia.com/vietnam_tourism.html).

25. Niezen, *The Origins of Indigenism*, 2. Niezen goes on to characterize the very term "indigenous" as "an expression of identity, a badge worn with pride." And the "Identities versus Globalization"

conference, sponsored in January 2005 by the Heinrich Böll Foundation in Berlin, singles out the "protection of cultural diversity" in a world where even the "languages of minority groups are disappearing" as the way to defend identity.

26. Franklin Foer, *How Soccer Explains the World: An Unlikely Theory of Globalization* (New York: HarperCollins, 2004), 4, 5. Foer and Huntington are not alone in their preference for what David Brooks, celebrating the death of "multiculturalist tribalism," calls "liberal nationalism" (*New York Times*, April 26, 2006). With respect to economic issues, of course, nothing hangs on which of these two forms of identity one prefers. Credit where credit is due, however: what attracts Brooks about what he thinks of as the new nationalism is its interest in "inequality" rather than "discrimination."

27. As Foer's own sports examples show. It's not as if having an international sports league requires everyone to root for the same team. In fact, it's just the opposite: if everyone rooted for the same team, you wouldn't really have a league; you'd just have the Harlem Globetrotters and the Washington Generals. Globalization isn't opposed to difference; it requires difference. But it also prefers that difference be understood just as Foer understands it—on the model of identity, on the model of sports. We don't root for one team against another because we think its beliefs are true and the opponent's are false. We don't, in other words, root for ideological reasons; sports teams don't have ideologies. We root for sports teams because they are ours.

28. The speaker is a professor of education at the Federal University of Amazonas, quoted in the *New York Times,* August 28, 2005.

29. This is what gives the current debate over immigration its particular force. People like Huntington want to keep Mexicans out of the country because they worry about the threat to American identity. Responding to Lionel Sosa's book, *The Americano Dream,* Huntington writes, "There is no Americano-dream. There is only the American dream," and, panicked by the rise of Spanish, he con-

cludes, "Mexican-Americans will share in that dream . . . only if they dream in English," which he thinks, because of their numbers and their location (he worries about Miami), they will never do (*Who Are We?* [New York: Simon and Schuster, 2004], 256). To this cultural chauvinism, pro-immigration activists plausibly respond with indignation. But antichauvinism here, commendable though it may be, is also an instrument of neoliberalism, since minimally restricted immigration is, in effect, a kind of insourcing: you can't send your car to China to be valet-parked, but you can bring the nearest equivalently cheap labor here.

30. George Will, "The Conservative Imagination," *New York Times,* February 26, 2006.

31. *New York Times,* April 5, 2006.

32. Maybe, for example, American workers, unhappy about the loss of their jobs to China and about the growing economic inequality in American life, should start considering the views of some of the Chinese who, even though they're gaining lots of the jobs we're losing, aren't all that happy about the growing economic inequality of Chinese life. In China now, "the state-run news media are abuzz with calls to make 'social equity' the focus of economic policy, replacing the earlier leadership's emphasis on rapid growth and wealth creation" (*New York Times,* March 12, 2006). And although the circumstances are very different, a version of the same phenomenon appears to be taking place in Japan, where, as the economy emerges from what a reporter for the Associated Press calls its "decade-long malaise," the growing "gulf between rich and poor" has been a "shock" to a country accustomed to thinking of itself as "middle-class and egalitarian" (Chiseki Watanabe, http://www.themoscowtimes .com/stories/2006/04/21/253.htm).

33. Trevor Johnston, "W(h)ither the Deaf Community?" *American Annals of the Deaf,* vol. 148, no. 5 (Winter 2004), 374.

34. *Pittsburgh Post-Gazette,* February 8, 2005.

35. Simi Linton, *Claiming Disability: Knowledge and Identity* (New York: New York University Press, 1998), 150, 151.

36. http://www.signmedia.com/info/adc.htm.

37. "Assimilationist education is genocidal," says Markku Joki-
nen, president of the World Federation of the Deaf, and "according
to the genocide definitions in the UN Genocide Convention, Deaf
children and adults suffer linguistic and cultural genocide every day
all over the world" (www.un.org/esa/socdev/anable/rights/ahc5docs
/ahc5wfdside.ppt). The language of genocide is obviously extreme,
and I don't mean to suggest that many people use it. It's worthwhile
noting, however, that the WFD claims membership in almost 120
countries and is recognized by the UN.

CHAPTER 6. RELIGION IN POLITICS: THE GOOD NEWS

1. The census report racializes health insurance statistics in the
same way it does the poverty rate. The rate of the uninsured for
blacks is 19.7 percent, for whites only 11.3 percent. And a 2005 report called *Closing the Gap: Solutions to Race-Based Health Disparities* (issued by the Applied Research Center in Oakland in
collaboration with the Northwest Federation of Community Organizations) tells us that "racial disparities in health constitute a national crisis. Equalizing mortality rates between African Americans
and whites alone would have saved five times as many lives as all ad-
vances in medical technology saved between 1991 and 2000." No
doubt, the gap between blacks and whites in insurance rates helps
account for the gap in mortality rates. But the census report also
tells us that the rate of the uninsured among people with annual
incomes under $25,000 is 24.2 percent and that among those with
annual incomes above $75,000, it's 8.2 percent. This gap is a lot big-
ger than the racial one (and given the disproportionately large number of poor blacks, it does a lot to explain the racial one). So why is
the national crisis the racial disparity in health care? Why isn't it the
economic disparity in health care?

It's not hard to produce an answer to this question. A special
report to the Kellogg Foundation, *Undoing Racism in Public
Health,* says it all. If the disparities in health are a function of racism, undoing racism will undo them. If the disparities in health are
a function of disparities in the delivery of health care to the rich and

the poor, the solution will not be fewer racist doctors but universal health coverage. And as the health-care inequalities increase, this point becomes more obvious. The recent Commonwealth Fund Biennial Health Insurance Survey reports that 41 percent of "working-age Americans with incomes between $20,000 and $40,000 a year were uninsured for at least part of the past year—a dramatic and rapid increase from 2001 when just over one-quarter (28 percent) of those with moderate incomes were uninsured." Its title is *Gaps in Health Insurance: An All-American Problem*. Maybe you just need a critical mass of suffering white people in order to begin to see that it's neoliberalism, not racism, that's the problem.

2. Addressing the ways in which "diversity theory enriches diversity practice," the Global Diversity Institute offers "Professional Certification for Diversity Practitioners."

3. Cardinal Joseph Ratzinger, *Truth and Tolerance* (San Francisco: Ignatius Press, 2003), 184.

4. Richard John Neuhaus, *The Naked Public Square* (Grand Rapids, Mich.: Eerdmans, 1986), 14.

5. Cardinal Joseph Ratzinger, with Vittorio Messoni, *The Ratzinger Report* (San Francisco: Ignatius Press, 1985), 163. "The Eucharist is life," the pope says, and "we cannot share this life with those who have such a different understanding of the Church and the sacraments."

6. Alan Wolfe, *The Transformation of American Religion: How We Actually Live Our Faith* (Chicago: University of Chicago Press, 2005), 82.

7. That's the difference between being a Christian and being an American. When Huntington adds our religion (Christianity) to our language (English) as the other fundamental component of American identity, he gets this exactly wrong. He may sound a lot like Neuhaus—they both speak approvingly of "Christian America"—but they are saying very different things. Huntington wants us to hang on to "Anglo-Protestant culture" as a way of resisting universality, a way of making sure that America remains different and so remains itself. Neuhaus's Christianity is like the pope's. He cares

about our Christianity not because it makes us who we are but because it makes us (he thinks) right.

8. The complaint about prejudice against fundamentalists is John J. Pitney Jr.'s in "Dean and the Fundamentalists," September 22, 2003, in the *National Review Online. The National Review* has returned to this issue several times, insisting that "conservative Christians" are "the one group you're allowed openly to hate" (Stanley Kurtz, April 28, 2005), as if what Pitney calls anti-Christianity were a form of racism. Altevogt's remark and Frank's commentary are in Frank, *What's the Matter with Kansas?* 158—59.

9. http://people-press.org/reports/display.php3?PageID=11.

10. Wolf, *The Transformation of American Religion,* 5.

11. Shailagh Murray, *Washington Post,* September 5, 2005.

12. Neuhaus, *The Naked Public Square,* 36.

13. Ibid., 180. Neuhaus's idea in adding the church and religious teaching to the Bible is to distance himself a bit from the Protestant reliance on scripture precisely because he's aware that simply pointing to what seems to you some decisive part of even the New Testament doesn't produce the distance from revelation that he thinks is necessary for public argument. The church—particularly the Catholic Church, with its tradition of argument from natural law—looks more promising. But it seems doubtful that natural-law arguments can get you far enough away from revelation to do the trick. Thomistic arguments against homosexuality, for example, which justify sexuality by linking it to procreation, have a hard time doing so without appealing to God.

14. Ibid., 148–49.

15. Ibid., 86.

16. Ibid., 86.

17. Ibid., 163.

CONCLUSION: ABOUT THE AUTHOR

1. Or maybe not. Paul Krugman, who in recent years has done more than anyone to try to make economic inequality visible, reports that "the nonpartisan Tax Policy Center estimates that this year the

99th percentile will correspond to an income of $402,306, and the 99.9th percentile to an income of $1,672,726" (*New York Times,* February 27, 2006).

2. The example is Dalton Conley's, describing what he calls "positional goods" (*New York Times,* May 29, 2005). For an excellent account of social class in the *New York Times,* see Chris Lehmann, "All Classed Up and Nowhere to Go," http://www.bostonphoenix .com/boston/news_features/other_stories/multi_3/documents/047. And, in a 1997 article that has just (i.e., as this book is going to the printer) come to my attention, Lehmann has a couple of completely on-target paragraphs criticizing what he calls the American left's "compulsion" to "recast questions of class as questions of culture" with the consequence that the problem of economic injustice gets redescribed as the problem of classism and the project of redistributing wealth gets turned into that of broadening "diversity workshops" ("Popular Front Redux?" *The Baffler 9* (1997), 19–29). To which I can only, belatedly, say Amen.

3. Ladd and Bowman, *Attitudes Toward Economic Inequality,* 15.

4. Bruce Bartlett, "Economic Class-Stagnation Bull," *national reviewonline,* June 13, 2005. He's citing the *New York Times* poll for the *Class Matters* series, and the Ladd and Bowman study for the American Enterprise Institute.

5. Ibid.

6. Anthony DePalma, "Fifteen Years on the Bottom Rung," in *Class Matters,* 119.

7. Robert Pollack, *Forward,* June 10, 2005.

8. The point is made in a manuscript currently in preparation.

9. Cary Nelson, *Manifesto of a Tenured Radical* (New York: New York University Press, 1997), 31. As the newly elected president of the American Association of University Professors, however, Nelson is already displaying an activism that is more on target than his literary criticism.

10. Michael Lind, *The Next American Nation* (New York: The Free Press, 1995), 144–45.

AFTERWORD TO THE 2016 EDITION

1. If the foreign born were an ethnic group, they would be the third largest in the country, in between Hispanics and Blacks. But, broken down by ethnicity, they account for a little under 9 percent of the Black population and, of course, much more of the Asian and Hispanic population.

2. http://www.nytimes.com/2013/05/07/us/suit-cites-race-bias-in -farms-use-of-immigrants.html

3. https://georgiafarmworkerrights.wordpress.com/2013/04/15 /american-farm-workers-sue-vidalia-onion-growers-for-not-paying -minimum-wage/

4. http://www.npr.org/sections/money/2014/10/02/349863761/40 -years-of-income-inequality-in-america-in-graphs

5. http://www.epi.org/publication/income-inequality-by-state -1917-to-2012/

6. http://money.cnn.com/2015/03/11/investing/wall-street-bonus/

7. http://www.npr.org/2014/05/05/309840501/remembering -economist-gary-becker-who-described-marriage-market

8. http://www.bls.gov/opub/reports/cps/highlights-of-womens -earnings-in-2013.pdf

9. http://www.bls.gov/oes/current/oes193032.htm#nat

10. http://www.nelp.org/content/uploads/Occupational-Wage -Declines-Since-the-Great-Recession.pdf

11. http://healthaffairs.org/blog/2015/08/11/reinventing-home -health/

12. http://www.bls.gov/news.release/union2.t02.htm

Index